Tradable Permits in the Transport Sector

Tradable Permits in the Transport Sector

Charles Raux
Laboratoire d'économie des transports, Lyons, France

Translated from the French by Kevin Riley

This book was published with the support of the *Direction de la recherche et de l'innovation* (research department) of the *Commissariat au développement durable* (ministry of ecology, sustainable development, transport and housing) in relation with the *Programme de recherche et d'innovation dans les transports terrestres* – Predit 4.

The publisher thanks La Documentation Française for its kind collaboration.

ISBN: 978-2-7420-0794-3

Éditions John Libbey Eurotext
127, avenue de la République
92120 Montrouge – France
Tel.: +33 1 46 73 06 60
Fax: +33 1 40 84 09 99

John Libbey Eurotext
42-46 High Street
Esher, Surrey
KT10 9KY
United Kingdom

Note on the Predit programme

Predit 4 (2008-2012) is a French programme for coordinating research and innovation policy in the area of land transportation. It is the result of an agreement between three French ministries (Sustainable development, Industry and Research) and three national agencies (ANR, ADEME and OSEO), uniting their incentive measures relative to land transportation (*i.e.* road, rail and waterways) in response to current social issues, notably with a view to sustainable development. Predit aims to further progress in knowledge, technologies and services in two key areas:

- making transportation systems more efficient,
- providing support for the definition and application of public policy in the area of transportation.

These general objectives are reflected in 6 priorities and six experts groups are each attached to one of these priorities:

- Energy and the environment
- Quality and safety of transportation systems
- Mobility in urban areas
- Logistics and freight transport
- Competitiveness in the transport industry
- Transport policies

Predit operates in close cooperation with various public and private-sector partners: industry, research bodies and universities, local authorities, transport operators and competitiveness clusters. Experts from these different partner organisations sit in the governance board for the programme and are involved in the experts groups.

Within the framework of international cooperation, Predit has developed special relations with its German equivalent, the « Mobilität und Verkehrstechnologien » programme, through the Deufrako cooperation initiative. With a view to constructing the European Research Area, Predit serves to develop strategies relating it to Europe's R&D Framework Programme and promote the involvement of French teams in this programme. Multilateral cooperation is being developed, mainly under the framework of the ERA-NET Transport platform.

Predit is chaired by a member of the French Parliament, presently Jean-Louis Léonard, MP for Charente-Maritime. A permanent secretary is held by the ministry in charge of ecology and transport (MEDDTL).

http://www.predit.prd.fr

Contents

Foreword

The issues raised by greenhouse gas emissions mean that it is high time for us to consider the potential of tradable permits in the transport sector. The first discussions on tradable emissions permits, in France at least, fell into a linguistic trap. This was partly due to the initial terminology which talked about a "market for the right to pollute". The very concept of the right to cause harm is quite naturally offensive. Not only can the idea of such a right be rejected as spontaneously as the idea of a right to steal or to attack someone, but matters are made even worse by the possibility of trading the right!

If we consider in detail the system required for the tradable permit mechanism, the vocabulary becomes still more aggressive: the initial allowance of polluting rights establishes an emissions cap and necessarily creates a system of rationing. Rationing a word that brings back painful memories of rationing coupons. Issuing coupons of this type would constitute a return for central government to a somewhat shameful former role, but by allowing them to be traded, the authorities obviously put themselves in an even worse position: would it not thereby be legalizing a "black market" and instantly laundering the revenue from it?

In a world where some people consider "market" to be a dirty word, there is no shortage of vocabulary for stigmatizing this system. Nevertheless, we can try to identify, dispassionately, the features that differentiate it from more traditional pollution control measures.

Whether it is based on instruments known as "permits", "rights" or "norms", there is nothing new about pollution emission thresholds: these are classical pollution control measures which are simply based on a norm. Obviously, this norm designates a prohibition: it is, for example, prohibited to make more than a certain level of noise with one's vehicle and breaking this rule should be penalized. But this norm also designates a right, as the threshold also defines a range of permitted emissions levels. Whatever term is used to describe it, *the "right to pollute" already exists. It comes into play as soon as a norm is selected to limit a given type of pollution and the value of that norm is not fixed at zero.*

In the traditional system, exceeding the norm is punishable, generally by a fine. The alternative is therefore to: comply or pay. This still applies in the tradable permit mechanism as an operator that is unable (or unwilling) to comply with the norm must purchase the corresponding permits from other operators who have not used all their emissions rights.

This is what the tradable permit mechanism and the traditional norm-based system have in common. We shall now see that they differ in two important respects.

The first difference relates to the cost of the violation for the polluter: with tradable permits, this cost is no longer dependent on a legislative decision but on a market price. This price cannot be lower than the lowest marginal cost of pollution abatement, as otherwise it would not be in the interest of sellers to do better than what is permitted by the norm.

The other difference is that the penalty for exceeding the emissions for which one holds permits, either allocated or purchased, must be much greater than in the case of an ordinary norm-based system. The severity of the penalty is accepted because of the possibility of purchasing rights and it is the general rule in tradable permit schemes.

Obviously, these differences in the mechanisms are responsible for differences in outcomes. One of the explanations for the observed effectiveness of tradable permit schemes resides in the severe penalties which apply to those who have difficulty complying with the law, as it becomes in their interest to try to do so. The other explanation relates more to the least constrained operators. In the ordinary norm-based system, an operator who has the opportunity of emitting less than the regulation authorizes at low cost has no incentive for doing so. However, once it is possible to sell unused permits, this incentive exists.

Thus, for a predetermined emissions level, there is a collective benefit if those emitters with very high pollution abatement costs can choose to finance an equivalent but less costly emissions reduction for another operator by purchasing permits.

So, compared with the norm-based mechanism, the tradable permit scheme in theory has the advantage that the same pollution abatement goal can be achieved at lower cost. Alternatively, the permitted emissions level can be lowered insofar as the risk of eliminating production units is lessened by their ability to buy permits. *In short, what is involved is exploring the least costly source of pollution abatement.*

The principal theoretical advantage of the tradable permit scheme over the pollutant emission taxation system is that it guarantees that the goal will be achieved, simply because the goal has been converted into a number of allocated permits while with taxation, achieving this goal depends on how demand responds to a certain level of taxation.

The comparison between tradable permits and classical instruments is given detailed coverage in the first chapter of this book. Nevertheless, we need to consider whether a scheme of this type is realistic for transportation. This issue is examined in Chapter 2 which provides some partial responses by considering some applications.

To go further, as Charles Raux attempts to do in the third chapter, it is necessary to tackle some difficult issues. These relate to the details of the system and the devil is in the detail. They also involve some recurring themes in the area of tradable permits: for example, difficulties with regard to monitoring, the terms of the initial allowances of permits or the costs of the scheme when in place. In the case of transport, these may present difficulties which raise doubts about the theoretical superiority of the tradable permit scheme over norm-based systems, taxation or even voluntary agreements.

As this book points out, there have been few applications of tradable permit schemes to the transport sector. The conclusive experiments have above all involved industries with limited numbers of pollutant emitters which are easy to monitor. Can these be transposed to highly fragmented transport activities? Should they be applied upstream, in vehicle manufacture for example, or a long way downstream, as near as possible to the end user?

For a number of years, Charles Raux has been leading groups of researchers at the Transport Economics Laboratory (Laboratoire d'économie des transports) who have been trying to shed light on these issues and explore the realms of the possible. This publication presents a summary of this research which is clearly at the forefront of our current knowledge. Having himself helped to build up this knowledge, Charles Raux is well aware of it and has succeeded in making it highly accessible.

Alain Bonnafous

Introduction

Why talk about "tradable permits" or "transferable quotas" in the context of transport? For a start, what are they?

According to the general definition given by Olivier Godard (in OECD, 2001), transferable permits are instruments whose function ranges from introducing flexibility into classical regulation to organizing competitive permit markets. These instruments have the following features in common: (1) they involve fixing quantified constraints (quotas); (2) these quotas (or rights) are allocated initially to agents independently of the environmental obligations imposed on them; (3) agents are able to transfer the quotas between activities or locations *(averaging)*, between different time periods *(banking)* or to other actors (*trading*, in the case of tradable permits); (4) they employ *ad hoc* penalties to ensure that the emissions behaviours of the agents match the rights or quotas they hold.

As Godard and Henry (1998) have observed, the introduction of emissions quotas does not create "polluting rights" but restricts these rights where previously they were unlimited. Making these quotas "tradable" then introduces flexibility and minimizes the total cost to the community of reducing emissions.

In what follows the terms "permit" and "quota" are used interchangeably. In the general case, we should talk about "transferable permits", but as permit schemes only become truly effective in the framework of an exchange market, we shall use the expression "tradable permits".

The most emblematic example of a tradable permit market for controlling pollutant emissions is the one for sulphur dioxide (SO_2) emissions from thermal power plants in the United States. These emissions are responsible for "acid rain" (the *Acid Rain* programme)[1]. Since 1995, power plants have received a number of SO_2 emission quotas each year, in proportion to the amount of energy they produce and a technical SO_2 emission norm fixed by the regulator. Power plants which exceed their quotas have to buy the missing permits on the market, while those power stations that emit less than their quotas sell their unused permits. Conducting transactions on the SO_2 emissions permit market is now part of the normal everyday activities of power station managers.

The European carbon dioxide[2] (or CO_2) Emission Trading Scheme (ETS), which came into being on January 1, 2005, covers energy-intensive facilities and provides another example

1. This programme is described in greater detail later in this publication.
2. This gas has many other uses, such as in carbonated water and drinks, not forgetting its uses in liquid form (carbon dioxide snow used in fire extinguishers) or in solid form (dry ice).

which is of more direct concern to European countries. At present, this programme covers approximately 12,000 plants in the European Union, but the European Commission wishes to bring the issue of transport to the fore and has recently proposed the inclusion of air transport in the ETS[3].

How could tradable permits schemes be applied to transport? Transport infrastructure and the associated services which permit the movement of persons and goods are key to the economic and social development of societies. However, when attempting to achieve these general goals, the transport system is currently subject to a number of major physical, environmental and financial constraints, as a consequence of present-day technology.

One example of this is road congestion which occurs at certain locations and at certain times, and is the sign of a scarcity of space for traffic because, for example, society is unwilling to increase road capacities, or when there is a shortage of public money to do so.

Another example is local or regional pollution, to which transport contributes, through the combustion of motor vehicle fuel. This includes "acid rain", photochemical pollution from ozone in the troposphere (at low altitude, which is responsible for respiratory problems) and the destruction of ozone in the stratosphere (where it protects us from ultraviolet radiation). To this are added a large number of pollutants that are harmful to human health such as carbon monoxide, highly carcinogenic volatile organic compounds, and microparticles[4] which carry a variety of toxic compounds deep into our lungs (CITEPA, 2006). Legal limits apply to most of these atmospheric pollutants: for example, Directive 1999/30/EC sets the maximum daily exposure limit for PM_{10} microparticles at 50 $\mu g/m^3$ in the European Union and the annual limit at 40 $\mu g/m^3$.

Finally, the question of climate change and greenhouse gas emissions from human activities is taking the front of the stage[5]. France has committed to a reduction by four of its emissions by 2050 relative to 1990 levels ("Factor 4")[6] while the UK Government has committed to an 80% cut. Because of its dependence on the internal combustion engine, in most countries the transport sector is one of the main sources of greenhouse gas emissions, particularly CO_2 coming from the burning of fossil fuels, one of the main greenhouse gases. Transport generated approximately 25 percent of emissions of CO_2 in the world in 2003, and this share amounted to 30 percent in OECD countries. Among the transport CO_2 emissions, 18 percent

3. These points are examined in greater depth below.
4. PM_{10} particles have a diameter of less than 10 µm, and $PM_{2.5}$ particles have a diameter of less than 2.5 µm and penetrate further into the lungs, even sometimes as far as the alveoli.
5. We are assuming that the reader is familiar with the topic of the greenhouse effect and climate change. Here are some books in French. For a short, clear and instructive introduction, see Le Treut and Jancovici (2001). A fuller presentation is available in another book by Jancovici (2002). For an overview see Jean-Marc Jancovici's website which has several pages in English: <http://www.manicore.com/anglais/documentation_a/greenhouse/index.html>
6. According to the IPCC, in view of the current increase in the atmospheric concentration of CO_2, a reasonable objective would be to stabilize the figure at 450 ppm (compared with 382 ppm today), to restrict the increase in average temperature to within a range of 1.5 to 3.9° C. To obtain this stabilization, the world would have to reduce global annual emissions in 2050 to 4 billion tonnes of carbon, i.e. 0.6 t of carbon per inhabitant per year. In the case of France, this represents a reduction in current emissions by a factor of 4, hence the "Factor 4" goal.

come from road transport; 3 percent from air and 2 percent from maritime transport (OECD 2007). The need for action in the transport sector is also due to the fact that transport exhibits one of the largest potential for emissions growth (together with the housing and tertiary sector): emissions from transport have increased by 31 percent in the world between 1990 and 2003. However, since 2000 the rise in oil prices and the following slowing down of economic activity have had a curbing effect on transport fuel consumption.

In addition, prospective studies agree that limiting the number of vehicle kilometres travelled is an indispensable part of the package of measures that must be implemented in order to limit the growth in transport emissions (see for example: Radanne, 2004; ENERDATA and LEPII, 2005).

The concept of sustainable development, particularly the recognition of the limited nature of environmental resources, means we have to overhaul completely the economic analysis of the environment, particularly the theory of external effects (Godard, 2005). This theory contains a conceptual asymmetry which compares the economic costs of reducing pollution (which are compensated for in the cycle of economic reproduction) with external damage caused by a net destruction of the environment, which has a further impact on the utility functions of agents. The trade-off between the economic costs of reducing pollution and external damage leads to a gradual erosion culminating in the complete destruction of the environment's ability to absorb pollution.

Consequently, we must no longer merely apply the "polluter pays" principle but include the cost of restoring the environment in the agents' trade-off, and this cost may be infinite. By imposing a quantitative constraint on the consumption of environmental resources, permit schemes are a natural response to the goal of sustainable development.

It is for this reason that we shall begin by briefly describing the principal theoretical findings which justify our interest in permit schemes, the history of their implementation and the lessons which can be drawn from it (Chapter 1). Chapter 2 then analyzes the relevance and potential of permit schemes in the transport sector which are then illustrated by a few examples of applications in this sector. Finally, some proposals based on recent research will be presented (See the chapter "The proposals").

Tradable permits: theory, experiences and lessons

The first section of this chapter will describe the theoretical considerations that underlie our interest in tradable permits. However, the theoretical argument alone does not suffice and the permit markets which have already been successfully trialled for several decades provide useful lessons which we shall examine in the second section. Finally, the third section will look at the fight against climate change by considering the early stages of the application of the Kyoto protocol and the European emissions trading scheme.

From theory to implementation

To understand fully the operation of quota markets, we first need to see them within the framework of a comparison between pure regulation and economic instruments that provide incentives for changing behaviours. We will then see that economic instruments such as taxes and permits each have their respective advantages and disadvantages. The practical implementation of permit schemes requires a number of decisions to be made whose consequences are analyzed. Last, we draw a conclusion about the essential conditions for permit markets to achieve economic efficiency.

The superiority of economic instruments over norms

The origins of the economic theory of pollution permit markets can be traced back to Coase's work (1960) on external costs, which was followed by that of Dales (1968) on the regulation of water use and that of Montgomery (1972) on the formalization of permit markets.

What conditions are required to minimize the total cost of reducing emissions?

To reduce pollutant emissions, or more generally reduce the consumption of scarce resources of a public good (*i.e.* air, the climatic equilibrium, urban space, etc.), three main types of instruments are available to us:

- a unified norm, for example limiting the unit consumption of engines or the amount of lead additive per litre of fuel;
- taxation, which consists of taxing the consumption of scarce resources, for example fuel taxes, charging for the drawing of water or for congestion;

• permit markets in which each actor must hold permits (also known as quotas) for the consumption of natural resources – for example emission permits – which the actors can trade amongst themselves.

Taxes and tradable permits are economic instruments for public action[1] which modify the economic environment of agents, be they households or firms, in order to encourage them to change their behaviour. They are incentive instruments insofar as the agents are able, in the case of transport for example, to reduce their vehicle-kilometres travelled or change their vehicle or fuel, etc. in order, ultimately, to reduce their pollutant or greenhouse gas emissions.

These economic instruments allow the authorities to avoid collecting data on the technologies, behaviours and costs of reducing the emissions of each agent. Large-scale operations of this type, which are costly and in some cases impossible, would be necessary in the case of regulations which set out to be as inexpensive as possible, that is to say a norm which is not unique but adapted to each agent. Economic instruments provide agents with the same signal price (the rate of the tax or the price of the permit) and the agents adjust their behaviours in a decentralized manner: this decentralized distribution of efforts is such that it minimizes the total cost to society of reducing emissions. Box 1 provides an intuitive presentation of this outcome.

Box 1. The economic efficiency of regulation instruments for the environment

Let us consider two firms A and B whose production activity causes each of them to discharge 1,000 tonnes of a given effluent (for example methane) into the atmosphere. Let us assume that the objective is to reduce total emissions of the effluent by 10%, *i.e.* 200 tonnes. The figure below shows the marginal cost curves[2] of a reduction in the quantities of effluent discharged (for simplicity these have been assumed to be straight lines) for firms A and B. The lines slope upwards, that is to say as more emissions are avoided, the unit cost of reducing emissions increases: the first units are easier and less expensive to avoid than the last.

Imposing a single norm on both firms consisting of a reduction of 100 units of effluent would have a marginal cost for firm A for the 100th unit saved of €2K and for firm B a marginal cost for the 100th unit saved of €0.667K. For both firms, the cost of this reduction would be equal to the area of the triangle delimited by the reduction cost curve and the vertical line consisting of the norm, *i.e.* €100 K for firm A and €33.3K for firm B. The total cost of reduction would be €133.3K.

The use of an economic instrument (tax or permits) provides a way of minimizing the reduction cost. In this example, in order to fix the level of taxation required to obtain a total reduction of 200 units of effluent, let us assume that the authorities know the reduction costs for the two companies. The same quantitative result as the norm could be achieved by applying a tax of €1K on each unit of effluent discharged. In view of its costs reduction curve, it is in the interests of each firm to reduce its emissions as long as its marginal cost of avoiding a tonne of emissions remains lower than the tax: it follows that firm A will reduce the amount it discharges by 50 units and firm B by 150 units, *i.e.* a total of 200 units. The overall objective is achieved, but at a lower cost: €25K for A and €75K for B, *i.e.* a total cost of €100K.

1. The interested reader may find a fuller presentation of international negotiations on greenhouse effect and the economic analysis of permits in a report drafted by Olivier Godard and Claude Henry for the Conseil d'analyse économique (1998).

2. The marginal reduction cost of a unit of effluent is the incremental cost of this reduction, and is expressed mathematically as the derivative of the total reduction cost with respect to the total reduction that is achieved. It varies according to the total level of reductions.

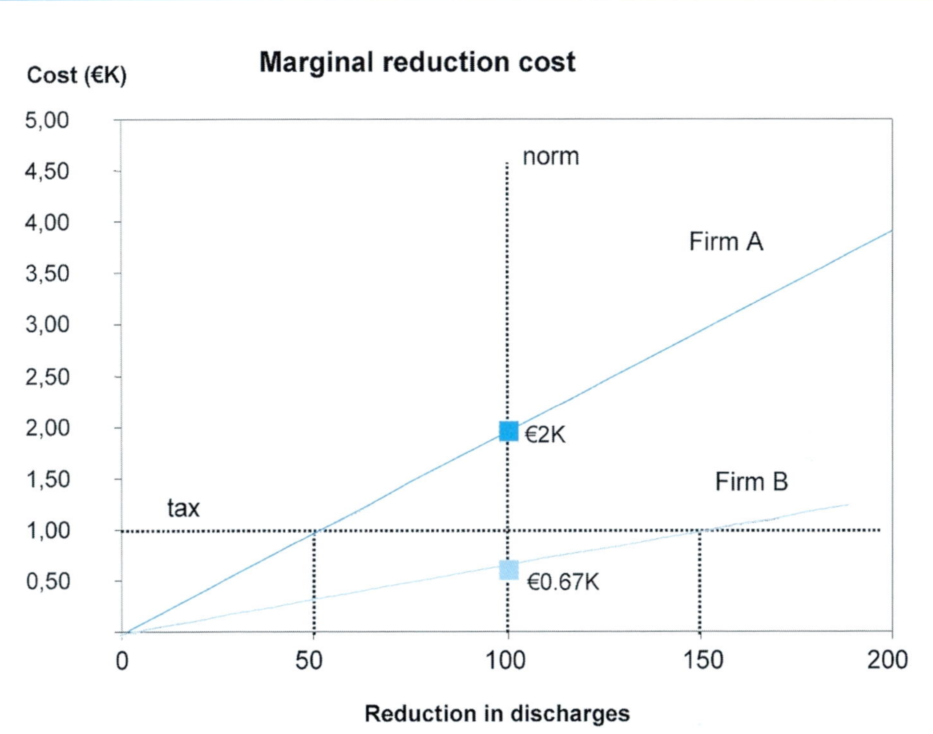

Another way of reducing emissions is to set up a permit market. Each firm is allocated a quota of 900 permits and a permit represents an authorization to discharge one tonne of effluent. Therefore, with the same reduction costs as in the figure above, the equilibrium will be established at the level where the price of the permit on the market is equal to the common marginal reduction cost of €1K. It will be in firm B's interests to reduce its emissions by 150 units (saving the 151st unit costs it more than €1K) and it will therefore discharge 850 units. It could then sell its 50 unused permits to firm A. It will be in firm A's interests to reduce its emissions by 50 units (saving the 51st unit costs it more than €1K) and emit 950 units. It will purchase the 50 permits it lacks from firm B at a price of €1K each.

	Reduction cost	Purchases/sales of permits	Total reduction cost
Firm A	- €25K	- €50K	- €75K
Firm B	- €75K	€50K	- €25K
Total	- €100K	€0K	- €100K

In this situation (in the case of known abatement costs), the same collective result is obtained by the tax and the permits, an emission reduction of 200 units at an overall cost of €100K.
Another important point to be noted is that the marginal costs of reducing emissions must be sufficiently different to encourage firms to trade, in order to draw benefits that exceed the transaction costs (see below).
(Adapted from Raux and Marlot, 2001)

As the economic efficiency condition applies to all emissions sources, there is no reason, indeed quite the opposite, for fixing a specific reduction objective for a given sector or a specific activity such as transport. This principle may be overridden on the grounds of social justice (for example lower taxation for domestic diesel oil), or because of international competition policy (for example, the partial refunding of the French domestic tax on oil products for road freight transport), or acceptability (for example, the European directive on emissions quotas which is restricted to major energy consumers). Derogations of this type are paid for by a reduction in economic efficiency.

Permits or tax, which instrument to choose?

With regard to the *quantitative reduction goal*, the essential difference between taxation and permits is due to the fact that in practice the authorities do not possess full information about the reduction costs for the different agents. The permit-based ("cap-and-trade") approach guarantees that the quantitative emissions reduction objective will be achieved but provides no guarantee concerning the level of the actual marginal costs of reduction. However, with taxation, the marginal reduction cost for each agent is fixed by the level of the tax, but there is no guarantee about the quantitative level of emissions reduction.

This uncertainty makes the choice a difficult one, as errors when forecasting harmful impacts or agents' reduction costs, and more particularly with regard to the distribution of effort over time and between sectors or agents, can be extremely costly for the community. There are, however, several criteria which can help us in this choice (Baumol and Oates, 1988).

The first criterion applies when environmental damage is likely to increase very rapidly with the level of emissions when certain thresholds are approached or exceeded causing extremely serious, irreversible, damage. In this case, tradable permits guarantee that the quantitative emissions limitation objective will be achieved. The problem of greenhouse gas emissions is a particularly good example of this.

Whether one chooses a tax or permits also depends on whether uncertainty applies to the real cost of pollution reduction, which may be the case in the transport sector.

For example, the following CO_2 emission reduction measures are possible with regard to personal travel: changing driving style; reducing vehicle-kilometres travelled (by having more occupants in the car, reorganizing journeys, changing locations of activities – holidays, leisure, shopping or personal business, work, home –; changing vehicle or changing to a transport mode that consumes less energy).

On two important points, namely changes in the locations of activities and changes in transport mode, the possibilities for action differ very greatly both in nature and extent according to the residential locations of the individuals (urban, suburban, rural). Changing the locations of activities in order to bring them closer together is considerably easier in urban areas than in suburban or rural areas, as a result of the density of the available activities: short term changes are possible in the case of activities with few location constraints, such as shopping or leisure: it is easier to reduce the distance between one's home and place of work in a conurbation which provides a high density of job opportunities. Likewise, the consolidation of flows that results from the increased density of activities means that public transport that provides a viable alternative to the private car is more frequently available in urban areas.

Therefore, everything points to the fact that the curves for the marginal cost of emissions reduction are extremely varied, and, in particular, are steeper as one moves from urban to suburban and then rural areas.

A similar analysis could be conducted for freight transport if one compares deliveries in urban areas with medium and long distance transport, and the possibilities of logistical adaptation and changes in transport mode.

In the context of such uncertainty and with regard to a quantitative objective for limiting the consumption of environmental resources, the permit scheme is still *a priori* advantageous.

However, the choice between taxes and permits cannot be made *ex ante* and requires a case-by-case analysis. A general solution to this problem of uncertainty as regards the costs of pollution abatement (*i.e.* emissions reductions) has been proposed by Baumol and Oates (1988, pages 74-76), based on an idea by Roberts and Spence.

If the regulator fails to put enough permits on the market (for a given year or a given sector), the free play of the permit market will lead to an excessively high price. The regulator can then introduce a tax *t* based on the principle that pollution emitters are authorized to emit more than the amount allowed by the permits they hold by paying the tax *t* for its additional emissions. In this situation, as soon as the price of permits exceeds the level *t*, it is in the interests of the emitters to pay the tax[3]. The upper bound of the price of permits will therefore be fixed by *t*. However, in order to comply with international commitments, the regulator may have to bear any disparity between the value of the domestic permit and its value on the global market.

Conversely, if too many permits are put on the market (as was the case with the ETS in 2003-2006), the free play of the permit market will result in a price that is too low. In this case, the regulator can introduce a buy-back price *r* for unused permits. Here, as soon as the price of permits falls below the level *r*, it is in the interest of the emitters to sell their unused permits. The lower bound of the permit price will therefore be fixed by *r*. However, in this case, the regulator must finance the buy-back of the permits.

This hybrid solution in which taxation and permits are combined is applied when the regulator has to take decisions, either about the temporal distribution of the reduction effort (for example, annual goals), or about the distribution of the effort between different sectors.

To sum up, uncertainty about the cost of pollution abatement justifies the setting up of a hybrid system which combines a permit allowance, a tax *t* and a buy-back price *r*. However, for the government, the risks associated with such mixed systems differ according to whether or not the market is open to the international permit market.

3. This is not the case for the European permits trading scheme (ETS, see below), as the penalty tax does not discharge the CO_2 tax liability.

Some practical considerations concerning implementation

In practice, the three principal questions to be answered are the following:

- What entities will be able to exchange quotas? For example, in a CO_2 emissions reduction programme, will these entities consist of those supplying fossil fuels upstream, or the end users of the fuel downstream?
- Should some quotas be allocated free of charge? If not, the entities covered by the programme will have to purchase all the permits they need on the market, which, in a situation where the total amount of quotas available on the market is subject to scarcity, is equivalent to auctioning quotas. This is the most economically efficient solution as it compels the players to reveal their preferences, without the costly data collection required by most distribution methods. It complies with the polluter-pays principle and also creates a financial resource that is usable in the context of a "double dividend"[4]. It is not discriminatory, particularly with regard to market entrants who are on an equal footing with the others, unlike some allocation methods (see below). However, from the outset, it increases the financial burden on the players involved, which explains their resistance. On the opposite, the fact that the permits are allocated free of charge reduces the tax burden on the agents and increases the acceptability of this instrument: in certain cases it is difficult to envisage making the consumption of a good which is considered to be free payable without visible or immediate compensation.
- If quotas are allocated free of charge, what distribution method should be used? Although in theory these methods do not threaten the efficiency of the instrument, they ultimately determine the financial burden which will weigh on the affected sector and the participating entities. The implications in terms of redistribution mean that the choice of the method is decisive for the acceptability of the programme.

While the answer to the first two questions depends on the specific application, allocation methods have general characteristics which transcend specific situations: for this reason, we shall now conduct a brief review of the benefits and disadvantages of the three basic methods which consist of allocation on the basis of past emissions, allocation according to a baseline and allocation according to a norm.

Allocation on the basis of past emissions

This method of allocation is frequently known as *"grandfathering"*. It entails allocating permits to polluters in proportion to their past emissions. It is this method which has been adopted for the European Emission Trading Scheme (ETS) that targets greenhouse gas emissions from energy-intensive plants and which has been running since 2005 (see below).

The main criticism levelled at this method is that it rewards poor performers: all other things being equal, those who use old polluting technologies will, as a proportion of their activity, be allocated more quotas than other more virtuous entities. Moreover, it encourages emitters

4. Both taxation and the permit system, due to the incentives they provide, are able to bring about a change in behaviours which will result in an effective reduction in emissions: this is the "first dividend". The "second dividend" is the result of the fiscal resources which may be provided by implementing these economic instruments. This fiscal resource could be used in other sectors of the economy, for example, to reduce social security charges.

to delay their pollution reduction activities as soon as they foresee the introduction of a system of this type, which generally takes several years to prepare. To overcome this problem, the regulator can go further back in time in order to calculate rights, or allocate additional quotas to those entities that voluntarily reduce their emissions before the system comes into force.

Strictly speaking, this procedure creates a barrier to those wishing to enter the economic activity covered by the permit scheme. The reason for this is that new entrants must generally purchase their quotas on the market, unless a free allocation mechanism is put in place for them with a quota reserve[5]. In this last case, we must expect firms to act opportunistically, creating subsidiaries to take advantage of these allowances.

Last, this allocation method requires the collection of data on each firm's past emissions. In the case of the European scheme, this collection is already done because of the notifications that are compulsory under the Kyoto protocol. However, if this is not the case, this type of data collection can be extremely costly, or even impossible.

Consequently, the administrative costs of calculating grandfather rights may be extremely high if there are too many emitting entities: "only" about 3,000 power stations are covered by the Acid Rain programme: for instance a programme covering all the firms in France would involve about 2.5 million entities, without counting administrations.

Baseline and credit schemes

An emissions baseline, initially calculated over a given period in the past, is fixed for each entity. If the entity emits less than this baseline level, it receives credits which it can trade on the market or bank in order to offset future emissions. The possibility of selling credits provides an incentive for the entity to improve beyond its baseline. If the entity emits more than its baseline it must buy permits on the market. Subsequently, the baseline may be reduced annually to encourage entities to make continual improvements.

This method has much in common with the previous one, grandfathering. Like grandfathering, it encourages poor performers to the detriment of good performers. The first are able to reduce their pollution more easily and therefore obtain credits. Like the previous method, it also requires data to be collected on each entity.

Here too, a variant of the system makes it possible to integrate new entrants with an *ad hoc baseline:* in this case, the risk is that the total limit for emissions will be exceeded.

Norm-based allocation

In this method, the regulator sets a technical coefficient for emissions, for example in comparison with best practice *(benchmarking)*, which reflects the programme's goal. Credits are then allocated with a reference to an *output* which reflects the entity's production of emissions. For example, in the "Acid Rain" programme (see below) the emissions allowances for

5. As some European countries have done in the framework of the ETS (see below). There is a danger with this variant that the limit for the total emissions of the sector in question will be exceeded, in that any new entrant will automatically increase the allowances. The *Acid Rain programme* in the USA (see below) is an example where different rules have been combined in order to avoid these negative side-effects.

each generating unit are calculated by multiplying the technical coefficient for SO_2 emissions by the average amount of heat produced by the power plant during a given period.

This system provides an incentive for power generators to adopt "cleaner" norms. In addition, the technical coefficient is lowered each year, in a way that is determined by the regulator.

In contrast with grandfathering, this method encourages virtuous actors, *i.e.* those who have undertaken pollution abatement measures earlier. Furthermore, it removes the entry barrier described above. In order to avoid an increase in total allowances as a result of new entrants, the technical coefficient may be adjusted for the subsequent annual allowances in order to maintain the same total allowance limit.

Last, in most cases, data collection is less expensive than for other methods, in that there is no need to reconstruct the production and emissions history of each entity.

The programmes that have been implemented in practice tend to be hybrids of these different methods in order to combine their advantages and minimize their disadvantages. However, it will be apparent to the reader that the way they cope with new entrants is an important issue for all three allocation methods. If we decide to provide free quotas to new entrants, it is very difficult to define precisely what we mean by new entrant, in order to avoid certain undesirable ways of getting round rationing. However, the problem of defining new entrants does not arise if they have to buy their quota allowance.

The debate between taxes and permits is usually presented as involving the two following equations: tax = fiscal resource on the one hand, and permit = initial free allowance = no fiscal resource on the other. However, in theory, there is nothing compulsory about these equations. In the case of the tax, the first units emitted may be subject to exemptions or relief on the grounds of acceptability or equity considerations. For the agents who are affected, these are equivalent to the initial free allowance in the case of permits. The tax revenue can also be refunded either to an entire sector or a branch on the basis of an emissions-neutral criterion such as the added value or the value of production. Conversely, the sale of permits instead of an initial free allowance may produce a fiscal resource similar to the standard mechanism of taxation. To sum up, both taxation and permits may provide similar responses to the double dividend problem and pose the same distributive problems.

Box 2 summarizes the principal characteristics of a cap-and-trade emissions scheme.

Box 2: The main characteristics of a cap-and-trade permit scheme

A cap-and-trade emissions permit scheme has six principal characteristics:

1. The regulator sets the total emissions quota for a given period within a given geographical area or for a given set of sources ("the cap").
2. The regulator determines the point of obligation, that is to say the entities which will hold the permits and return them to offset their emissions.
3. The regulator sells permits or distributes them free of charge to the entities, for example on the basis of their past emissions or efficiency norms, within the limits of the total quota that has been set. Each permit authorizes its holder to emit a specified quantity of pollutant.
4. The entities are authorized to trade permits amongst themselves. Those entities whose emissions reduction costs are lower than the price of the permits on the market are encouraged to reduce their emissions below their initial allowance and sell their unused permits.

5. At the end of the period, each entity must return the number of permits that corresponds to its emissions. Entities are therefore able to comply with regulations either by reducing their emissions or by buying permits.
6. One of the fundamental conditions for the efficiency of these schemes to be efficient is the rigour of the procedure for measuring and checking emissions and the regulatory and penalty system: an entity which emits more than is allowed by the permits it holds must receive large fines.

It is of course obvious that the practical details of a permit market have impacts on the effectiveness and the competitiveness of its operation, as well as on transaction costs.

The conditions for the economic efficiency of tradable permits

Generally speaking, the economic efficiency of a permit programme will be achieved, whatever the initial allowances, if certain conditions are met (Baumol and Oates, 1988):

- provided that the reduction functions are convex over their relevant value ranges, the equalization of the marginal costs of reduction between all the sources is a necessary and sufficient condition for minimizing the total reduction cost of aggregate emissions for a given reduction target;
- a tradable permit scheme equalizes the marginal reduction costs for all the sources as soon as it allows the optimum allocation of emissions permits between them: the equilibrium allocation of emissions permits (and hence the distribution of reduction efforts) will be the same whatever their initial allocation;
- in the absence of transaction costs, perfect information concerning reduction costs is not needed for achieving the quantitative reduction goal, contrary to the determination of the correct level of taxation.

Consequently, permit markets make it possible to separate issues of efficiency from issues of equity more easily than is the case with a tax.

Two other criteria should be taken into consideration when choosing between taxes and permits, as they have a direct influence on the total cost of reducing emissions: these are the transaction costs that may be involved in permit trading and whether the permit market operates in a competitive or a non-competitive manner.

The reason for this is that transaction costs fundamentally change the issue of separating efficiency and equity. Stavins (1995) has identified three types of transaction costs:

- those linked to the acquisition of information on the alternatives available to actors and finding trading partners;
- costs associated with negotiation and decision-making (consulting brokers, length of the negotiations, legal aspects, insurance);
- the costs linked to monitoring and compliance with rules, which are in principle met by the authorities.

Stavins has modelled the impact of transaction costs and shown that the initial allowance of rights affects the final balance and the total costs of reducing emissions. The authorities must therefore attempt to minimize transaction costs, in particular by avoiding finicky regulations, such as the need for each exchange to have administrative approval, which hamper transactions (see the examples given by Hahn and Hester, 1989; see also Foster and Hahn, 1995).

They must also reduce the costs of finding information and the cost of uncertainty for the actors on the market, either by behaving as an active broker between vendors and purchasers or by facilitating the activities of private brokers.

It is therefore important to design a simple system whose administrative costs are as low as possible.

In addition, some firms could be able to exercise market power, in particular by preventing other firms from entering the permit market. These market concentration and strategic behaviour issues mean that less trust can be placed in systems with narrow markets (Stavins, ibid).

However, contradictory conclusions are reached concerning the advantages and disadvantages of markets with a limited number of actors and markets with a large number of actors. "Small" markets may be more vulnerable to strategic behaviours but allow easier transactions between actors who know each other, one example being the permit market for lead additives in petrol in the United States (see below). On the other hand, "large" markets are less vulnerable to strategic behaviours and can also make transactions easier as the probability of finding a partner for an exchange is greater.

More recently Crals and Vereeck (2005) offered a definition and an in-depth comparison of transaction costs between taxes and tradable permits. Transaction costs include legislative, information, search, set-up, operational, negotiation, contract, monitoring and enforcement, and compliance costs. Their conclusion is that the overall costs depend on the details of the scheme design, whether tax-based or permits-based.

SOME INSTRUCTIVE EXAMPLES

The first use of quota markets involved levies on natural resources, water pollution and air pollution.

Quotas for natural resources

There have been many local examples of the trading of rights to draw water in a number of countries, particularly the United States, Australia and Chile. These have mostly involved the distribution of water for irrigation purposes or making trade-offs between agricultural and non-agricultural use of water resources.

As regards fishing, the trading of rights or quotas is a long-standing practice in some countries, not only for river fishing but also in some periods for sea fishing, particularly whaling: an agreement dating back from 1932 between British and Norwegian whaling companies fixed quotas for the number of whales that could be caught and limited the whaling season in the Antarctic.

From the outset, these quotas were designed to be tradable, although their price was not fixed at the outset. Several countries (Australia, Canada, Iceland, the Netherlands, New Zealand,

and the United States) have used this instrument in particular since the 1970s for a variety of species including tuna, lobster, herring and sole.

The principle of fishing quotas is widely applied in the European Union common fisheries policy. The total catch authorized by the Commission is split between the Member States, which then allocate quotas to the fishing vessels registered under their jurisdiction. The transfer of quotas between Member States is authorized, although flexibility in this area is not unlimited.

With regard to the management of land use and the regulation of building activities, experiments in transferable building rights have been conducted in the United States since the start of the 20th century. The most significant applications from the environmental standpoint were launched at the end of the 1970s and the beginning of the 1980s in France and in New Zealand. In France, the Urban Planning Code specifies that the local urban plan may determine, in areas which must be protected because of the quality of their landscapes, the possibilities for transferring building rights between land in a given zone with a fixed floor area ratio in order to group buildings together.

Water pollution rights

There are currently dozens of local water pollution rights programmes running in the United States. The first such programme began in March 1981 in Wisconsin on a roughly 60 km section of the lower reaches of the Fox River which received effluents from about 10 pulp mills and 4 municipalities. Only a single transaction took place in this rights trading programme as a result of major restrictions: those purchasing rights had to prove their need, the rights were limited by the terms of the vendor's permit (a maximum of 5 years), and trading required administrative approval.

Another project involved water pollution rights at the Dillon Reservoir, a mountain lake in Colorado (Hahn and Hester, 1989). This rights trading programme was launched in 1984 and related to phosphorous discharges. Rights were awarded on an annual basis. In order to increase its discharges, a point source (*i.e.* a water treatment plant, a ski resort, etc.) had to purchase rights from so-called "non-point" sources (*i.e.* septic tanks, suburban areas, etc), which put in place measures to reduce their discharges. The programme placed few restrictions on trading.

Experiments of this type were restarted by the United States Environmental Protection Agency (USEPA) in 2003, and the programme to improve water quality by means of tradable permits is now running and managed by a specialized network (the Environmental Trading Network), that was set up originally for the Great Lakes region.

Air pollution rights

The Unites States' *Clean Air Act* of 1990 was a response to previous failures with regard to air quality and marked the first stage of the introduction of a genuine market for rights to emit SO_2, which causes acid rain. This market began to operate in 1995. It concerned SO_2 emissions from thermal power plants operating within the United States which at the time were responsible for 70% of SO_2 emissions. The goal was, from the year 2000, to reduce emissions from the electricity sector to half their 1980 level, *i.e.* approximately 9 million tonnes per year.

The *Acid Rain* programme created a new market covering a large geographical area[6]. The rules for the initial allocation of rights (which were free for existing sources) were fairly complex, and involved a large number of situations in which entities were awarded additional rights. Permits were allocated on an annual basis and could either be used immediately or banked for later use, or even sold to any purchaser. Regulation of this market was both rigorous, as regards rights allocations, the monitoring of emissions, the recording of account activity and the setting of penalties, and flexible with regard to the transactions, in which the administration took no part. In 2000, it was commonplace for power station managers to carry out transactions on the SO_2 permit market.

It took some time to gradually convince the different parties (firms, environmentalists and even administrations) of the economic benefits of this instrument and its environmental robustness. The programme's success shows how powerful the regulator must be in order to manage a system effectively.

Last, the Acid Rain programme is a good illustration of the scale of the disparities between the costs that are estimated *ex ante* by experts in the strategic framework of negotiating a new policy and the costs which actually emerge *ex post* once adequate incentives have been put in place to encourage innovation. Although these costs are not comparable with the price of the transactions, they were overestimated *ex ante* by at least a factor of two compared with the ex-post effective costs. There is therefore no reason for not thinking that the benefits of this kind of scheme might be considerable with regard to the prevention of global climatic change.

The general criteria for the success of a permit scheme

Experience of implementing tradable permit schemes means we can identify a number of general criteria for success (from OCDE 1997, 1998).

First, of course, there must be broad agreement about the need to act, the effectiveness of the scheme with regard to improving the environment and its lower cost compared to other schemes or solutions. In addition to this, equity must be considered (particularly for allocation methods), as, more generally, must social and political acceptability.

The first major criterion for the scheme is simplicity and clarity. The target must be clearly identified (for example, the amounts of SO_2 emitted) and the unit of exchange must be defined, easily measurable and verifiable. The rules for allocating and exchanging quotas must be simple in order to keep transaction costs down. The institutional and geographical boundaries of the market and participants must be clearly identified.

A second criterion, which is just as important to the efficiency of the scheme, is the possibility that the market will function. There needs to be a sufficient number of agents who are willing to take part in the market and they also need to be able to pay the probable price of the permits. In addition, the anticipated marginal costs of pollution abatement must be sufficiently different for gains to be made through trading.

6. The description below is taken from an article by O. Godard (2000) on American experience of tradable permits which appeared in *Économie internationale*.

Last, the scheme's efficiency depends on the credibility of emissions monitoring, verifications and the rigour with which penalties are applied. Also, in order for economic agents to optimize their behaviour in the long term, it is essential to be sure about the future validity of the permits.

THE HESITANT BEGINNINGS OF THE KYOTO PROTOCOL AND THE EUROPEAN TRADING SCHEME

By signing the Kyoto protocol, which was drafted in 1997, the majority of developed countries accepted legally binding targets for reducing the six major greenhouse gases[7]. The European Union is committed to reducing its emissions by 8% between 2008 and 2012 (the first commitment period)[8], compared with 1990, and has distributed the effort between its Member States in the framework of the "European bubble").

The Kyoto protocol came into force in February 2005 after ratification by at least 55 countries responsible for 55% of the emissions from industrialized countries[9]. This ratification opened the way for the implementation of the three flexibility mechanisms proposed under the protocol. These are, apart from permits ("emissions rights") that can be traded between countries, the two project mechanisms which allow a country or a firm to obtain certified emissions credits in exchange for funding a project that leads to emissions reductions, either in a country liable for reducing emissions ("joint implementation") or in a developing country (the "clean development mechanism")[10].

As the European Union wanted to provide good example to other countries, in particular industrialized countries, it was among the first to set up an emissions rights trading scheme (the *European Trading Scheme*, ETS) that operates between European firms. This scheme has been operational since January 1, 2005, but so far only applies to combustion plants with a thermal rating of over 20 MW (*i.e.* about 10,000 plants across the EU). Consequently, it mainly, but not exclusively, involves industrial firms that either consume or produce a large amount of energy (*i.e.* mostly the production of ferrous metals, cement, glass, ceramics and paper). The only gas covered at present is CO_2 and the ETS in this first phase covers around 40% of the EU's total CO_2 emissions. Applying the directive and the principle of subsidiarity[11], it is the Member States which allocate quotas to the firms in question: each State has to submit a national allocation plan (NAP) to the European Commission)[12].

7. The six greenhouse gases in question are carbon dioxide (CO_2), methane (CH_4), nitrous oxide (N_2O), hydroflurocarbons, (HFC), perfluorocarbons (PFC) and sulphur hexafluoride (SF_6).
8. The objective of the protocol is to achieve an average reduction of 5.2% for all industrialized countries, whereas the 1992 Rio convention targeted a reduction of 50%.
9. With the notable exception of the United States and Australia, while rapidly developing countries such as China, India and Brazil were not among initially concerned by the protocol.
10. One example is for an industrial country to finance the replacement of a fleet of buses in a developing country.
11. This was an inappropriate application of the principle of subsidiarity as the system would have been efficient if an allocation had been decided at European Union level (Godard, 2004).
12. However, the Directive set a common penalty level for the case where a firm exceeds its quotas, and this penalty of €40 per tonne of CO_2 was not a payment in full discharge.

An analysis of the implementation of this directive in France (Godard, 2004) has shown that allocation of the quotas was particularly lax, providing a classical example of the capture of public decision-making by a major industry, which was allowed because of a desire not to impair the competitive positions of the firms: as a consequence, the firms are subsidised through generous free allocations, including those which were intended for the expansion of activities and new entrants, which means they face virtually no constraints. Consequently, the micro-economic incentive for trading, which is what makes the scheme efficient, is absent.

Despite this laxity, of which most of the other Member States were also guilty, observers were surprised by the price tension affecting the quotas during the first months of operation: the *spot* price for a tonne of CO_2 rose from €8.5 to almost €30 in July 2005, and then varied between €20 and €25. Electricity producers were responsible for most of the purchases, on the one hand because of circumstantial factors (2005 was a cold winter, and there was an increase in the use of coal, which emits more CO_2, in response to an increase in oil and gas prices), and some precautionary buying caused by uncertainty about future economic growth and constraints on carbon use (Alberola, 2006). In 2005, it is estimated that 12% of the 2.2 billion quotas allocated in Europe were the subject of transactions.

In early May 2006, following the Member States' first reports of their actual emissions during 2005, the price of the quota on the spot market fell to €8.5, and then rose to about €15 during the summer of 2006. The market successfully provided a price signal in the situation where there is an abundance of quotas, in a situation of uncertainty regarding the value of these first period quotas during the second period from 2008 to 2012. When it became clear that the allowances held in this first phase would not be valid during the second phase (2008-2012) the market price collapsed again with prices plummeting to less than €1 in 2007.

In order to avoid a situation of this type re-occurring in the second phase of the ETS (2008-2012), the European Commission imposed a 10% reduction in the total emissions from the Member States and succeeded in obliging several States to toughen up the first versions of their emissions plans.

The revision of the ETS post 2013 was validated during the year 2008. The capping of EU 27 Member States industrial emissions is set at 21% below 2005 levels by 2020. The scope is enlarged to new industrial sectors, two new greenhouse gases and aviation (see below). It is expected that 50% of all EU emissions will be covered. A common distribution method for free allowances based upon benchmarking of most efficient techniques and processes will be set up at the European level (Euractiv, 2009). Moreover, from 2013 auctioning of emission allowances will be introduced and increased with the aim to have 100% auctioning in 2027. Sectors not included and which use fossil fuel, such as ground transport or buildings for instance, are expected to achieve a 10% reduction of emissions on their own by 2020: national caps have been established for these sectors.

Relevance for transport and some applications

Permit markets have some interesting features, as the examples we have briefly examined have shown. But can they be transposed to the transport sector?

We shall start to answer this question by analyzing the relevance of these mechanisms for transport and describing their potential with respect to the various adverse impacts and the possible targets. We shall then present and draw lessons from a few current or past permit schemes in the transport sector.

How relevant are these schemes for transport?

Compared with the economic instruments that are already used in the transport sector, permit schemes have several points of special interest [1], particularly with regard to regulating the sector. The four most important of these are as follows:

- A certain level of uncertainty applies to the price response function of agents, as we have seen above. For example, in the case of CO_2 emissions, fuel demand has a low price elasticity in the short and medium terms which means a quantitative goal would be more easily achieved by a permit scheme than by taxation.
- In view of the high level of fuel taxation in Europe, agents would perceive permits with a free allocation as a means of escaping an additional tax, which might help improve the acceptability of the new instrument.
- As we have already seen, quota schemes are the only way of dealing explicitly with distributive aspects independently of the problem of the economically efficient allocation of efforts to reduce environmental harm. In view of the fundamental role of transport with regard to the right to travel, special attention needs to be paid to how these distributive impacts are dealt with.
- With regard to the flexibility of the implementation of the regulation policy, permit schemes (like tolls) provide a way of targeting the local and regional problems caused by transport.

In addition to these general aspects, the transport sector has some characteristics which make it particularly suited to permit schemes. Two principal criteria enable us to decide whether

1. Cf. OECD (2001)

or not permit schemes are appropriate. These are, on one hand, the possibility of establishing a constraint or a right which is defined quantitatively within specified spatial and temporal limits, and on the other hand the possibility that agents will be able to trade some or all of these quantitative obligations.

In many cases, it is possible to set precise and measurable quantitative goals: this is the case with greenhouse gases emissions from transport for which goals can be set for each agent as it is the sum of the individual outputs of agents which produces the total output. Where greenhouse gases are emitted is of little importance at a planetary level, so these emissions are equivalent at this planetary level, and quotas may be traded at a regional, continental or even planetary level.

The existence of threshold effects may also make a quantity-based approach necessary. An obvious case is greenhouse gas emissions, but it can also be applied to local or regional atmospheric pollutant emissions, for which concentration threshold values must not be exceeded on health grounds. In this last case permits may be traded within an appropriately sized zone. In all these cases, it is the sum of the agents' individual outputs which produces the total output, and it is fairly easy to establish spatial and temporal equivalences for the total amount of pollution[2]. However, this is not the case with noise which does not increase linearly as a function of individual emissions.

Congestion is usually restricted to specific corridors or network nodes and at specific times. However, in the case of conurbations or urban regions where congestion occurs over long periods of time and large areas, quota schemes for road travel can be envisaged (see below).

The main argument against the use of permit schemes in the transport sector concerns the administrative cost of these schemes, which, by definition, target a large number of mobile sources. From this standpoint, if the target can be linked with fossil fuel consumption with a sufficient degree of accuracy (as in the case of CO_2, for example), the extension of existing fuel taxation naturally appears as the least costly solution. In other cases, such as congestion, the use of the electronic moving vehicle identification technology used to collect road tolls seems to be the most appropriate solution. In addition, this technology, which is being applied more and more, can provide a means of reducing the administrative cost of some permit schemes (see the case study on Ecopoints in Austria below). Resolving the issue of administrative costs is of central importance for any implementation of tradable permits in the transport sector. We will see how this issue can be dealt with in the case studies below.

Furthermore, the introduction of permit schemes in the transport sector would make the rationing of the activity via its outputs, *i.e.* trips, explicit. This may threaten the freedom to travel, and this is a fundamental right that is universally recognized in Declaration of Human Rights such as that of the United Nations. This threat stems from the car's irreplaceable role in travel.

A priori, it is not clear which of tax or permits is less socially acceptable. Fuel taxation would seem to play more of a silent role, as it is included in the final price the consumer pays, but

2. If we consider only primary gases. The secondary chemical reactions which may follow, such as for example the formation of tropospheric ozone are not considered. One reason for this is that gaseous masses may be carried over large distances.

it would have to be at a higher level than it is today to achieve the goal of reducing greenhouse gas emissions.

Last, compared with pure regulation on its own, tradable permits would introduce the idea of market transactions with regard to the universal right to travel which we have mentioned above: in some cultural contexts, this may constitute an additional disadvantage for tradable permits compared with uniform regulation.

In what precise areas of the transport sector could tradable permit schemes be applied?

The overall emissions output of transport activity is the outcome of a combination of factors related to land use (the location of activities and its impact on travel distances), the supply of infrastructure and services (the price and quality of service for the different transport modes), the technical characteristics of the transport vehicles (energy source, unit consumption, emissions) and the level of vehicle use (the level of travel as a function of economic and social activity). These factors all provide potential areas of action for regulating pollution from the transport sector.

The first potential area we shall consider relates to land use, particularly the attempt to limit urban sprawl and the dispersion of activities which lengthen travel distances: the longer distances in question are generally travelled by private car, the public transport alternative being unavailable in low density areas. Currently, this is an area where regulation is mainly applied, but there have been proposals to create tradable building rights for property developers based on the traffic volumes generated by their projects (Ottensman, 1998).

The second area concerns household vehicle ownership. A mechanism that rations vehicle ownership has been implemented in Singapore since 1990 (Koh and Lee, 1994), in addition to the road tolls for the central business districts and the major roads in this "city-island-State" that have been operational since 1975. Rationing is based on the auctioning of a limited number of certificates of entitlement to purchase (and import) a new vehicle (Singapore does not have any domestic car production). The number of certificates is set each year by the government, on the basis of traffic conditions observed and road capacity. These certificates are auctioned each month. Chin and Smith (1997) have shown that this mechanism is an effective means of controlling car ownership, as demand is relatively inelastic and the gradient of the social cost of car ownership is steep: the result is that compared with control by prices, control by quantities reduces the loss in overall welfare which would result if the authorities make a poor assessment of the optimum.

The third area involves vehicle technology, via the regulation of vehicle unit emissions of local atmospheric pollutants or greenhouse gases, and the technical characteristics of fuels. As we shall see below, this approach has been successfully applied in the United States in order to phase out the use of lead as a petrol additive and also includes the most sophisticated proposals that apply to motor manufacturers (see below).

The fourth area relates to the total amount of fuel consumed by vehicles, on the basis of their unit consumption and level of use. We will see that the limits that apply to fuel taxation lead us to explore the feasibility of permit schemes that target fuel consumption.

Finally, the fifth area, which is related to the previous one, also involves limiting vehicle use, or more precisely vehicle kilometres travelled (VKT), as a means of remedying congestion. Queuing is still the main way of regulating congestion, despite on-going debates about congestion charging which have been stimulated by the implementation of the London congestion charge in 2003 and the successful introduction of the Stockholm congestion tax in 2006. It could therefore be valid to introduce permits for quotas of VKT (or trips) in a given conurbation which would be allocated to motorists and which they could trade (see next chapter).

If we cross tabulate the three major categories of adverse impacts, namely greenhouse gas emissions, local and regional pollution and congestion, with the targets we have mentioned above, we obtain *Table I* which shows the relevance of permit markets for various targets.

Table I. *Relevance of permit markets according to the adverse impacts and targets*

Targets Adverse impacts	Unit emissions or vehicle technology	Physical and chemical characteristics of fuels	Household vehicle ownership	VKT or trips	Final fuel consumption	Land use
Greenhouse gas emissions	**		*	*	***	**
Regional pollution	**	**	*	*	***	**
Congestion			*	***		**

from * = low to*** = high relevance

If our target is the reduction of greenhouse emissions, we must bear in mind that vehicle unit emissions are only one component of total transport emissions. Another component is the level of vehicle use, *i.e.* VKT: the latter could also be regulated by a permit market but, like rationing fuel consumption, this would have the disadvantage of rationing travel, while being less directly linked to emissions[3]. For this reason, final fuel consumption seems to be the most appropriate target: amongst other things, it would leave an opportunity for travel, allowing households to choose vehicles with lower emissions or use other transport modes.

Regulating land use is an intellectually seductive approach to achieving this goal of reducing greenhouse emissions, but it is controversial: it has not been proved that it is possible, by compacting today's sprawling cities, to reverse the tendency to travel longer and longer distances. Proponents will maintain that, on the contrary, the spatial concentration of activities provides more opportunity for mass transport, which is cost effective for the community and less polluting. Last, targeting household car ownership is another possible way of regulating the level of emissions, but the link with real consumption is too weak to make this an effective and acceptable target.

For local and regional pollutants, our conclusion concerning the relevance of the various targets is similar to that for greenhouse gas emissions. However, targeting the physical and

3. Unless we consider the technology of fossil fuel combustion to be fixed.

chemical characteristics of fuels (for example lead additives in the United States, see below) represents another way, in addition to the unit emissions target, of reducing the amount of harmful exhaust emissions produced per kilometre travelled.

Last, with regard to congestion, the most efficient incentive targets the vehicle-kilometres travelled by the user or even the number of trips in specific corridors (*i.e.* bridges or tunnels). The regulation of land use can also be an appropriate way of reducing VKT, while rationing car ownership is only an indirect way of reducing the level of car use.

The fact that a complex regulation system already exists in the transport sector means that it is necessary to consider how a tradable permit scheme will be integrated within this system. We shall see in the case studies how permit schemes are able to complement existing regulations.

SOME EXAMPLES OF APPLICATION IN THE TRANSPORT SECTOR

The programme to remove lead from petrol in the United States is an example of the successful application of tradable permits. The programme involved the trading between refineries of rights to use lead as an additive and was applied between 1982 and 1988 in order to speed up the phasedown of lead from petrol, prior to a total ban that came into force in 1996.

The second example we shall consider is the "Ecopoints" scheme for heavy goods vehicles passing through Austria. This is a non-tradable permit scheme that ran from 1992 to 2006 in order to kerb rises in pollutant emissions from HGVs in the Alpine region of Austria. Although the permits are not transferable, the experience gained from this application averts us to some potential advantages and disadvantages of permit schemes when they are applied to mobile sources such as HGVs.

The third case study is the Californian *Zero Emission Vehicle* (ZEV) programme. This is a scheme which aims to reduce the level of local atmospheric pollution caused by car use, by increasing the proportion of very low emission vehicles sold by vehicle manufacturers in California.

The lead phasedown programme in the US

This programme, which ran from 1979 to 1996, set out to eliminate the use of lead, which is toxic, as a petrol additive in the United States. The programme of rights transfers between refineries which was in operation between 1982 and 1988 speeded up the removal of lead additives from motor vehicle fuels, until a complete ban came into force in 1996. The literature contains many studies of this case (Hahn and Hester, 1989; Kerr and Newell, 2001; Kerr and Maré, 1998; Nussbaum, 1992; for a review see Raux, 2002).

Lead is one of substances added to petrol to increase the octane rating and reduce engine knock. Its properties were discovered by engineers at General Motors in 1921 and its use rapidly became universal. The toxicity of high doses of lead has been suspected, if not known, since the time of Ancient Rome. But it was only after the enormous increase in its use due to the rise of the car that the first scientific proof of its toxicity, even in low doses, was provided in the 1960s and 1970s: as a result, the use of lead came to be seen as a threat to public health (Lewis, 1985).

The second reason for phasing out lead in petrol had to do with the use of catalytic converters, which are incompatible with lead in fuel. Catalytic converters started to be introduced by American motor manufacturers from 1975, in order to reduce other emissions associated with fuel combustion (hydrocarbons, carbon monoxide and nitrogen oxides). This requirement also explains the decline in consumption of leaded petrol, as the automobile fleet was gradually renewed.

The use of lead as a petrol additive is now banned in most OECD countries. However, it is still widely used in Africa, Central and South America, Asia and Eastern Europe. In many of these regions, unleaded petrol was not available until recently (Kaysi *et al.*, 2000). The main reason for continuing use of leaded petrol is that it is the least expensive way of increasing octane ratings[4].

The different stages of the programme

Flexibility was introduced into the lead phasedown programme in three stages: the first consisted of *averaging*, the second of *trading*, and the third of *banking*.

In 1973, the EPA proposed new regulations to reduce, over five year period, the average lead content of all the fuels (leaded and unleaded) produced every quarter by each refinery: this average amount was to be reduced from the habitual level of approximately 2 g per gallon to 0.6 g per gallon in 1978. This was the first stage in the introduction of a degree of flexibility in the application of the standard, which was no longer applied to each gallon but to the average of all the fuel produced in a three-month period.

New scientific evidence about the toxicity of lead prompted the EPA to tighten up the standard in 1982, to a maximum level of 1.1 g per gallon, which was now calculated on the basis of the total amount of leaded petrol produced by the refinery. To facilitate this adjustment, a programme was introduced to allow the trading of rights to add specified amounts of lead to petrol.

Each refinery received rights on the basis of the amount of leaded petrol it produced: for example, a refinery that produced 100 million gallons of leaded petrol during any quarter of 1983 or 1984 when the standard was 1.1 g per gallon, received rights to produce 110 million grams in that quarter. If the refinery added less than the authorized amount of lead, it was allowed to sell its rights to the unused lead. If, on the other hand, it wished to add more lead than the standard allowed, it would have to buy additional rights.

The difference between the rights that each refinery held (or purchased) and the rights it needed had to be calculated every quarter and had to be either positive or null. The validity of the rights was limited to three months.

4. The alternatives consist of replacing lead by ethanol or methanol, which are very expensive, or of modifying refineries to use other procedures (catalytic reforming, alkylation, isomerization) in order to increase the octane rating of petrol.

The permitted level of lead in petrol was further reduced to 0.5 g per gallon in mid-1985. The EPA announced that the programme for trading rights between refineries would end in 1986 and that the norm in that year would be lowered to 0.1 g per gallon. At the same time, the EPA introduced the banking of rights, with the possibility of using banked rights until the end of 1987. In anticipation of the tightening of the rules, the refiners added less lead in the first two quarters of 1985 than they were authorized to, in order to bank rights for use in 1986.

In 1988, after the rights trading programme was wound up, the level of 0.1 g per gallon was applied to each refinery individually. Lead was completely banned as a fuel additive for road vehicles in 1996.

The characteristics of the programme

The norm as regards the amount of lead that could be added to petrol, which was laid down by the EPA, applied to all the refineries. However, participation in the rights trading programme was optional.

No prior approval was required from the EPA in order to trade the permits, but each refinery had to submit an *ex post* declaration every quarter regarding the amount of petrol it had produced and the amount of lead it had used. Those refineries that took part in trading and banking also had to mention in their declaration the amounts involved and name the refineries with which they had traded permits.

Overall, the transaction costs as identified by Kerr and Maré (1998) were not insignificant: they included the cost of optimization, the cost of seeking a partner and researching prices, the cost of uncertainty about the validity of permits that were in practice traded before they were validated at the end of each quarter by the EPA, the costs of negotiation and the costs of disclosing confidential information about refinery output. These costs explain why the smaller refineries tended not to take part in trading.

Appraisal

Cost savings for the refiners from the trading and banking programme have been estimated at several hundred million dollars (Hahn and Hester, 1989). Ultimately, the programme is seen as having been successful as the total amount of lead that was authorized was not exceeded and it enabled some refiners to adjust and remain operative, which they would not have been able to do without the flexibility provided by the scheme.

To summarize, this programme had three fundamental characteristics each of which is essential for the success of a tradable rights programme:

- the permit unit was precisely defined (a gram of lead) which eliminated any ambiguity about what was being traded or banked;
- the rules were simple and allowed a great deal of freedom in trading;
- the programme and its components were implemented pragmatically.

Another positive factor that facilitated implementation of the programme was the availability of affordable technological solutions for replacing lead in petrol. In addition, the consumption of leaded petrol was already on the decline as a result of changes in the vehicle fleet. The tradable rights programme served to speed up the reduction in lead use.

The Ecopoint programme in Austria

The Ecopoint programme, which ran until the end of 2006, was a non-tradable permit scheme that aimed to limit pollution and noise emissions from lorry traffic passing through Austria. Analysis of this programme is interesting because it shows how a permit scheme applied to mobile sources can protect a given region.

Austria is located at the crossroads between Central Europe's transit routes. The North-South route between Italy and Germany passes through it as does one of the major routes between Eastern and Western Europe, on which traffic is growing at a considerable pace[5].

Austria is a particularly mountainous country so North-South traffic is channelled through environmentally fragile Alpine valleys, particularly the Brenner Valley. The shape of these valleys means that exhaust emissions cannot readily escape and intensifies highway noise. The concentration of oxides of nitrogen is three times higher than on a plain with the same traffic volumes. The Brenner Valley carried 60% of North-South traffic in 1999.

Concern about this growing pressure on the environment led Austria to negotiate an agreement with the European Economic Community in 1992 which set out to reduce noise and atmospheric pollution from lorries passing through Austria. In 1995, when Austria joined the European Union, this agreement was confirmed as a derogation to the Single Market provisions which oppose all trade barriers between Member States. As the Ecopoint programme applied to all Member States, it did not fundamentally contravene the principles of non-discrimination and the harmonization of competition.

The programme

This agreement between EEC and Austria set up a system of transit rights known as Ecopoints ("Ökopunkte") for loaded or empty heavy goods vehicles (HGVs) with a gross weight of more than 7.5 tonnes passing through Austria. The system applied to HGVs from all European Union Member States and some other countries that had signed agreements with the European Union.

The target was the NOx emissions produced by HGVs with a gross weight of over 7.5 tonnes. The initial goal stated in the agreement was to reduce these emissions by 60% as compared to the reference year of 1991 over the twelve years for which the agreement was to run, *i.e.* by 2003. These emissions were represented by a quota of points, known as Ecopoints, which had to be used by HGVs to pass through Austria, with this quota being reduced in a linear manner each year on the basis of the reduction goal stated above.

The programme considered the unit HGV emissions which were stated at the time of manufacture. An Ecopoint corresponded to the emission of 1 gram of NOx per kilowatt-hour (kWh). For example, a vehicle that normally emitted 104 g of NOx per kWh would have to use 10 Ecopoints to pass through Austria.

Initial allowance

The Ecopoints were distributed among the Member States by the European Commission according to an allocation scheme established in the regulations and periodically revised by

5. Most of the data presented here is taken from CEC (2000), apart from a few Internet resources.

the Commission. Countries were then responsible for redistributing the Ecopoints, which remained valid for one year, between their national hauliers.

The allocation of Ecopoints between countries was based on their share of the traffic through Austria in 1991. The scheme did not cover HGVs making journeys to or from Austria or remaining within Austria. In practice, Italy and Germany used two-thirds of the Ecopoints while the third largest user was Austria itself (15%).

Countries that did not expect to use all their allocated Ecopoints had to return any unused points before October 15 of their year of validity. The Commission was then able to redistribute these points to other States in accordance with the proposals of a committee made up of the representatives from all the Member States. Ecopoint transfer was therefore not performed through a market, but took the form of an administrative procedure between all the participating States, that was limited to unused Ecopoints.

NOx emissions were targeted in order to encourage the use of progressively cleaner trucks. However, another objective was to reduce noise. In order to avoid a situation where NOx emissions were reduced while an increase in transit traffic occurred, a special quantitative limit was imposed on transit trips from the outset, the so-called "108% clause": if the number of transit trips in any given year exceeded that of the reference year 1991 by more than 8%, the number of Ecopoints distributed in the following year had to be cut by 20% beyond the projected linear reduction.

This happened in 1999 and sparked a dispute between Austria and the other Member States in 2000. This was settled by the European Commission which suspended application of the clause. According to this clause, many countries (including Germany, the main user of Ecopoints), would have used up their quota by the summer of 2000, meaning that hauliers from these countries would no longer have been able to pass through Austria. This crisis, which was marked by demonstrations in Austria on the Brenner motorway against the increase in HGV traffic, led to a reassessment of the programme and proposals for reform from the European Commission.

After much legal activity (in front of the European Court of Justice) and political wrangling, new temporary regulations were adopted according to a joint decision procedure involving the European Parliament and the Council of Ministers, in spite of the opposition of the Austrian government and Austrian members of the European Parliament.

This regulation extended the system of quotas to 2004 and until 2006, when the new Eurovignette Directive was to be implemented[6]. The limitation of the number of through journeys ("clause 108%") was abolished, the "cleanest" HGVs which used 5 points or less were no longer subjected to the quota system while most of the vehicles using more than 8 points were banned from travelling through Austria.

Monitoring and auditing

When Austria joined the European Union and internal border controls were abolished an electronic system for processing Ecopoints was introduced. This detected heavy vehicles with

6. After fruitless negotiations on this topic, a compromise was reached between the Parliament and the Council: a new Directive which amends the Eurovignette Directive was promulgated on 17 May 2006 (Directive 2006/38/CE)

the aid of an onboard device known as an "Ecotag", which was an early version of the onboard device used for road pricing for HGVs in Germany and Switzerland. Installation and operation of the electronic system was contracted out to a private operator.

In practice, more than 95 percent of Ecopoints were managed electronically. Paper Ecopoints had to be cancelled by the driver in machines located at the main points of entry to Austria. Random checks were performed on the paper Ecopoints of vehicles travelling inside the country.

About 4% of trips reported by Ecotag involved unauthorised use, and perhaps half a million fraudulent Ecopoints were used each year. However, there are no data on fraud by vehicles not fitted with an Ecotag.

Lessons

In terms of benefits, there was a very clear technological training effect. The proportion of HGVs (measured by number of trips) paying 15 Ecopoints or more fell from 51 percent in 1993 to less than 2 percent in 1999[7]. The average number of Ecopoints used by HGVs from Member States therefore declined more rapidly than the target set in the agreement. Although it is impossible to say exactly what role the Ecopoints system played in this technological change, it is probable that the system increased and accelerated the impact of the general programme for tightening European emission standards (EURO I, II and III).

One of the main criticisms levelled at the programme is that it provided insufficient coverage of pollution sources, as it did not cover HGVs making journeys to or from Austria or remaining within Austria. Another criticism is that it was excessively comprehensive for a measure aiming to preserve the Alpine valleys as it applies to the whole of Austria: this would permit a huge increase in through traffic and hence emissions in the Alpine valleys if this was offset by reductions in the plains.

However, instructive lessons can be drawn from this case study. First, the Ecopoint system showed that it is technically feasible to apply a quota-based permit scheme to mobile sources within a defined area. It thus provides a partial response to the frequently raised objection that the administrative costs of permit schemes for mobile sources would be too high.

Providing a region with fuller protection from polluting vehicles would require many more electronic detection gantries: a trade-off would have to be found between the costs and benefits involved, depending on highway geography. A system of this type would only be realistic in certain geographical situations (for example in valleys with few entry and exit points) or in tunnels or mountain passes.

Tightening emissions quotas in order to control traffic growth would create a disparity between the physical basis of the quotas (pollutant emissions) and the target (traffic) that could give rise to allocational inefficiency. An alternative might be to use trips rather than NOx emissions as the target. This would have the advantage of keeping the tax base simple, which is indispensable for a properly functioning system. It would also do more to encourage the use of rail as an alternative for crossing the country, which explains the Swiss proposal for an Alpine Crossing Exchange (see below).

7. The Euro III Standard that came into force in 2000 corresponds to a maximum of 5 Ecopoints.

The ZEV (Zero Emission Vehicle) programme in California

The ZEV programme (Zero Emission Vehicle) seeks to speed up the introduction of electric vehicles in order to reduce local atmospheric pollution in the State of California. It includes a system of credits based on averaging. These credits can also be transferred between manufacturers (trading) and over time (banking).

In the 1970s there were often more than a hundred smog alerts in the Los Angeles region in a year. A major effort was made to tighten up vehicle emissions standards, and emissions were reduced by 98 percent. Smog alerts declined sharply, to the point where there were none at all in 1999.

However, the California Environmental Protection Agency considered that more should be done as almost 95% of California residents lived in areas whose air quality did not meet US federal standards. Cars and trucks were the second most important source of atmospheric pollution (accounting for more than 50 percent of smog precursors). About one million vehicles are sold every year in California, which is the world's eighth largest economic area and the largest automobile market in the United States.

As it is forecast that the coming decades will see a huge increase in VKT, progress as regards the pollutant emissions[8] from petrol vehicles would seem to be a blind alley, as they will never be completely clean. The only answer seems to be the widespread use of Zero Emission Vehicles (ZEV).

ZEVs are defined as vehicles with no exhaust emissions, no evaporative emissions and no emissions as a result of their fuel production (for example the refining and distribution of petrol). Moreover, there had to be no risk of the onboard emissions control system deteriorating over time. Consequently, the only current candidate technology is the electric vehicle.

The California Air Resources Board (CARB) is the government agency in California responsible for monitoring air pollution, regulating emissions from motor vehicles and other mobile sources, and enforcing the measures in question.

The programme

The first major drive towards a large-scale reduction in pollutant emissions from motor vehicles in California dates from the early 1990s. From the outset, this programme applied the principles of averaging-based permits, while setting a highly ambitious goal for the introduction of electric vehicles. The programme has since undergone several amendments that have introduced a degree of flexibility into the forced march towards the ZEV objective, while maintaining that goal despite pressure from motor manufacturers[9].

The CARB drew up the LEV I (Low Emission Vehicle) programme in 1990. From the outset, the California LEV programme was seen as a complement to the federal exhaust emissions reduction programme (CAFE, see Box 3), but one that applied more rigorous norms in the context of the devolution of powers to the State level.

8. In this context, the main greenhouse gas, CO_2, was not considered to be a pollutant.
9. An important source of information is the CARB web site, at <www.arb.ca.gov/msprog/zevprog/zevprog.htm> The main references used in this section are CARB (2000a, 2000b, 2001) and Friedman et al. (1998). For a detailed review see Raux (2002).

Box 3. The CAFE programme in the United States

The Corporate Average Fuel Economy programme (CAFE)[10] provides incentives for the manufacturers of passenger cars[11] and light commercial vehicles[12], to improve the energy efficiency of their fleets as measured in *miles per gallon (mpg)*. This programme was introduced in the mid-1970s and is administered by the Department of Transportation (National Highway Traffic Safety Administration – NHTSA) while per gallon mileages are measured by the USEPA.

A manufacturer's CAFE rating is determined on the basis of the entire fleet it puts on the US market, by calculating the sales weighted harmonic mean. The programme applies equally to domestic, European and Asian manufacturers. The standard is fixed annually by the Automotive Fuel Economy Standards (AFES) which must be met by both domestic and imported fleets. The penalty for noncompliance is $5.5 per vehicle per 0.1 mpg under the standard. Manufacturers who perform better than the standard can bank their bonuses in order to make up for deficits in future years. They are also able to obtain CAFE credits by manufacturing vehicles that use alternative fuels such as natural gas or electricity.

This programme therefore resembles a system of non-tradable but bankable permits. It should, however, be noted that a system of this type does not prevent an increase in total emissions if there is an increase in the number of vehicles on the road or vehicle mileages.

Greene (1990) has shown that between 1978 and 1989 the CAFE standards had a much greater effect than petrol prices on the fuel efficiency of the fleets of American motor manufacturers.

In 1985, Ford and General Motors asked the Federal Highways Administration to relax the AFES standard on the grounds that they were liable to have to pay hundreds of millions of dollars in fines. This was done and the standard was not raised to its former level until 1990. Exceptions were also sought for light trucks whose sales dropped sharply in the 1980s with the result that the quota system failed to operate (Wang, 1992).

The LEV I programme was designed both to enforce more rigorous emission standards and give motor manufacturers greater flexibility as regards the use of fuels, pollution control techniques and type of propulsion. It came into effect in 1994.

The programme employed the Zero Emissions Vehicle (ZEV) concept, and established four categories of LEV: transitional LEVs (TLEVs), LEVs, ULEVs (Ultra LEVs) and ZEVs. Each category was defined according to a maximum emissions level for hydrocarbons (NMOG, non-methane organic gases), carbon monoxide and nitrogen oxides. The NMOG index was used as a reference indicator for total emissions of atmospheric pollutants.

Instead of requiring every vehicle sold to meet a single emissions standard, motor manufacturers are allowed to spread their fleet between the four vehicle categories and comply with the standard on the basis of a weighted average of emission rates for their entire fleet[13]. They can also earn credits if they exceed the specified norm and then sell or bank them. Alternatively, they can purchase credits if their fleet does not meet the norm.

10. Source: <http://www.nhtsa.dot.gov/portal/site/nhtsa> (consulted in October 2006).

11. For carrying 10 persons at the most.

12. For carrying freight or passengers with a gross vehicle weight rating of less than 8,500 lbs, i.e. about 3.86tonnes.

13. This weighted average is calculated for each manufacturer by distributing its fleet between 4 categories and applying the maximum permitted emissions rate for each category to the number of vehicles belonging to it that are sold.

Manufacturers who offer more ZEVs for sale than required in any model year earn ZEV credits. These are expressed in grams of NMOG per mile. They are calculated by subtracting the number of ZEVs required from the number of ZEVs delivered for sale, and multiplying this balance by the average NMOG emission standards required for the manufacturer's light-vehicle fleet (cars and light commercial vehicles). It is also possible for manufacturers to earn a credit multiplier for vehicles delivered for sale prior to 2003. A manufacturer can comply with the regulations by returning a certain number of ZEV credits, either earned previously or purchased from another manufacturer.

Manufacturers who are unable to offer the required number of ZEVs for sale or who fail to return the required number of credits, and do not make up the deficit within the specified time limit (one year), will be fined under the Health and Safety Code. This fine can be imposed on any manufacturer selling a new motor vehicle not compliant with the State emission standards, and amounts to US$5,000 per noncompliant vehicle. The number of noncompliant vehicles is calculated on the basis of the ZEV credit deficit.

Finally, a requirement was issued that required a minimum percentage of ZEVs to be delivered for sale. The initial legislation required the 7 largest vehicle manufacturers (American and Japanese)[14], to ensure that at least 2% of the vehicles they had on sale in California were ZEVs in 1998, with this percentage set to rise to 5 percent in 2001.

All motor manufacturers apart from "low volume" vehicle manufacturers come under the ZEV mandate and are therefore compelled to take part in the credits programme. The CARB is also responsible for certifying vehicles and auditing the credits returned by manufacturers. On the other hand participating manufacturers have full freedom in negotiating credit transfers.

The automobile and oil industries, along with elected politicians, brought pressure to amend this legislation, resulting in the March 1996 memorandum of agreement: the CARB agreed to push back the 1998 deadline to 2003, but in return insisted that the requirement for ZEV sales should be increased to 10 percent at that date. As well, through voluntary agreements negotiated between the CARB and each of the large volume manufacturers, the latter undertook to produce a certain number of demonstration vehicles between 1998 and 2000. For example, Mazda, one of the large volume manufacturers, in which Ford owned a one-third stake decided to buy ZEV credits from Ford in order to meet the minimum production targets for demonstration vehicles.

This regulation was again amended in 1998, in recognition of the difficulties vehicle manufacturers were experiencing in producing low-cost ZEV vehicles, and the wide diversity of technologies available for further reducing emissions (in particular, hybrid electric vehicles and fuel cell vehicles). The LEV II programme also introduced additional flexibility, in the form of partial ZEV credits which could be earned by producing "very clean" but not strictly ZEV vehicles. These partial ZEV credits were for Super Ultra Low Emission Vehicles (SULEVs), petrol vehicles which had to be certified to meet emission standards for 150,000 miles, and had to produce no evaporative discharges.

14. To begin with these were General Motors, Ford, Chrysler, Nissan, Honda, Toyota and Mazda. Mazda has since joined the "intermediate volume" manufacturers.

Underlying this reform was the CARB's recognition of the great progress that had been made in the emissions levels of very clean petrol vehicles: as their operating range was greater than that of electric vehicles, they had the potential to achieve greater market penetration, while bringing about a faster reduction in emissions. The requirement for emissions to be guaranteed for 150,000 miles[15] provided an additional guarantee of durable benefits.

At the end of 2000, only the Nissan Sentra (a SULEV), introduced in November 1999, had been certified for PZEV credits. Three other SULEVs introduced in 1999 and 2000 failed to obtain this certification (in particular because of the evaporations criterion).

In spite of growing consumer interest and a subsidy of US$5,000 to manufacturers for every ZEV sold, the manufacturers had virtually ceased production. There are two essential reasons for this: cost, fairly obviously, but also uncertainty in the absence of a guaranteed market and a definitive regulatory signal from the State of California.

The 2003 ZEV target was again confirmed by the CARB in January 2001 with, however, some amendments to reduce the programme's cost to manufacturers. Amongst other changes, as of 2007 the authorities decided to include Sport Utility Vehicles (SUVs), pick-up and light vans when calculating the required percentage of ZEVs, thereby increasing the calculation base by 50 percent. The CARB also set up an $18 million subsidy fund for consumers as an incentive to purchase or lease ZEVs (up to a total of US$9,000 for a three-year lease prior to 2003, and up to US$5,000 after 2003): these subsidies are additional to other local or federal incentives.

Appraisal of the programme

This appraisal relates to estimates of operating costs and the programme's anticipated benefits. After this, we shall briefly describe the positions of the various stakeholders in the debate about the development of the programme.

The administrative cost of the programme includes the CARB's measurement and monitoring of pollutant emissions, keeping track of new developments in engine and battery technologies, evaluating the impacts of the regulations on air quality and adjustment costs and, last, checking the credits returned by manufacturers. Only the last of these costs is specific to the credit programme, the others being an inherent part of any regulatory system. For this reason we can state that the additional administrative cost of the credit programme is fairly low.

However, the costs arising from the accelerated market introduction of electric vehicles are quite another matter (CARB, 2000a). Battery-powered vehicles were still significantly more expensive at the time of this appraisal, even if we consider various hypotheses regarding rising petrol costs or improved battery life. Only when volume production is reached (more than 100,000 vehicles per year) will high-efficiency electric battery powered vehicles achieve costs per mile comparable to those of hybrid vehicles or PZEVs.

15. In order to avoid the deterioration which affects conventional vehicles: ageing and contamination of the catalytic converter, malfunctioning of the emissions control system, alterations or lack of maintenance by the user. Periodic inspection programmes are perceived as not being able to prevent such deterioration.

The benefits are thus essentially in the long term, reflecting the slow rate at which electric vehicles are achieving market penetration. However, the programme has stimulated intensive research and development by federal agencies and private business, as witnessed by the filing of a large number of patents.

In terms of CO_2 emissions, the performance of electric vehicles depends on how the electricity is produced. Currently, an electric vehicle powered by electricity produced in California emits about 250 g/mile of CO_2, compared to 300 g/mile for conventional gasoline vehicles[16]. This advantage is less obvious, however in comparison to a diesel or natural gas vehicle (less than 270 g/mile) and disappears completely when compared to a latest-generation hybrid vehicle.

The participants in this debate fall into three main categories, namely the vehicle manufacturers, the fuel industry and environmentalists.

Although they do not present a united front, the manufacturers are primarily worried by what they see as excessive interference in their affairs and because they think they will be forced to produce vehicles at a loss. They feel that by introducing partial credits (PZEV), the CARB has implicitly recognized that there is no market for ZEVs and is therefore providing a means to get around the regulations. In their view, the CARB should admit this and abolish the ZEV mandate. In response, the CARB has refused to withdraw the ZEV mandate, and stated that PZEV credits are a way of giving manufacturers greater flexibility and encouraging the nascent ZEV industry.

The oil industry sees no benefit from the ZEV mandate, which represents a threat to its business, and it has therefore been strongly against the programme. In contrast, the natural gas industry is very interested in the PZEV system, because it can produce fuel for SULEV vehicles. The electricity industry is torn between disappointment over the reduction in the required percentage of ZEVs, which means lower future demand for electricity, and the hope of increasing sales from the compression of natural gas.

The environmentalists are divided between those who think that this further flexibility will reduce opposition by the 2003 regulatory deadline, and those who think that allocating credits to petrol vehicles, even "ultraclean" ones, will lead to an increase in total pollution.

Outlook

It is still too early to say whether the programme is a success, as its full impacts have only been felt since 2003. Until now, credit transfers have been limited to meeting manufacturers' voluntary commitment to produce demonstration vehicles in 1998-2000.

In addition, the transition from very clean petrol vehicles (such as SULEVs) to electric vehicles does not constitute a valid response with regard to CO_2 emissions in view of the way electricity is generated in California, but this was not the aim of this programme. However, by greatly reducing emissions from petrol vehicles by using SULEVs and hybrid vehicles (HEVs), the programme has indirectly led to enormous improvements in unit CO_2 emissions from vehicles with internal combustion engines.

16. Or 155 g CO_2/km for an electric vehicle.

The Californian example has shown that systems involving permits that can be traded between vehicle manufacturers may be completely viable, as the administrative costs are only very slightly higher than for a conventional regulatory programme.

The real difficulty in the Californian ZEV programme has always been getting vehicle manufacturers to disclose the real costs of research, development and production for electric vehicles. This situation is a classic example of information asymmetry between a public regulator and private sector economic actors. This type of programme requires strong political will in order to find a compromise in all cases which is acceptable to the motor manufacturers, but this political will is underpinned by public opinion which is very sensitive to local atmospheric pollution.

California's governor, Arnold Schwarzenegger, committed the State in September 2006 to adopting a programme to reduce greenhouse gas emissions by a quarter by 2020 and subsequently by 80% by 2050 compared to 1990 levels. The project includes the setting up of a permit scheme similar to the European one. Transport will also be included in this reduction plan, which follows on from the ZEV programme. Several other American States stated that they intended to follow the Californian example. The focus of the ZEV programme is now being shifted, adding GHG emission reduction to pollutant emission reduction (CARB resolution in 2009).

What has been happening in Europe? A voluntary agreement was signed between the European Automobile Manufacturers' Association (ACEA) and the European Commission in 1998. This agreement set out to achieve an average emissions level of 140 g of CO_2/km for new vehicles sold in 2008, which is less ambitious than that of 120 g of CO_2/km (*i.e.* an average of 5 litres/100 km for a petrol car) initially sought by the European Commission in 2005. Similar agreements were also signed with the Japanese and Korean motor manufacturers (JAMA and KAMA). Some see these agreements as a collective concession which motor manufacturers accepted in the hope of escaping real constraints.

The European Commission, anticipating that this voluntary agreement would probably not be complied with by 2008 or even 2012, has expressed its dissatisfaction. In 2005 it financed a study to introduce quotas for vehicle unit emissions (IEEP, 2005). However the emission trading approach for carmakers was not adopted by the Commission which chose the combination of a binding target for new cars, burden sharing between carmakers, and CO_2 fines. The binding target has been set at 120 g/km by 2012, to be achieved partly by the carmakers, which will have to meet a goal of 130 g/km, while the remaining 10 g/km will be achieved with other technical improvements such as biofuels or fuel-efficient tyres. Within this overall CO_2 emissions target of 130 g/km the limits for new vehicles will vary according to the mass of the vehicle (limit value curve). A carmaker will have to ensure that the average emissions of all its new cars are below the average permitted by the limit value curve. In this way, a carmaker can average out emissions within its own fleet of new cars, but it can also pool its emissions with other carmakers. CO_2 fines have been set for carmakers which exceed their CO_2 limits, with an increase from €20 per gram of CO_2 that each car emits over the limit in 2012 to €95 in 2015.

After intense negotiations in 2007 and 2008, under strong pressure from the car industry, with divisions between carmakers and thus between countries (French and Italian carmakers on average produce smaller and more fuel-efficient vehicles than German carmakers), a compromise was finally adopted in December 2008. The CO_2 emissions limit will be introduced gradually: in 2012, 65% of each carmaker's new fleet will have to comply with the average set by the limit value curve, with this percentage increasing by intermediate steps to 100% in 2015. Lower fines have been set for small excess emissions: €5 for the first g/km of excess, €15 for the second g/km, €25 for the third g/km, and €95 for each subsequent g/km (EC, 2009).

The proposals

A number of proposals have been made for dealing with local and regional problems raised by transport. We shall therefore present a brief survey of proposals for trip credits in order to control congestion, sum up the potential of parking quotas and examine a fairly sophisticated proposal for an Alpine Crossing Exchange for road freight.

However, the issue at the forefront is the possibility of using permit markets to limit the greenhouse gas emissions from transport. To begin with, it is necessary to analyze two major aspects of the design of mechanisms of this type, namely the choice of the target and the choice of the entities that hold the permits. We shall then describe and analyze four proposals: the first relates to air transport, the second to the allocation of carbon quotas to individuals, the third to motorists and the last to freight transport.

Trip credits for controlling congestion

In order to control congestion on a road or in a zone, one possibility might be a permit scheme for quotas of vehicle-kilometres travelled (or trips), which would be allocated to drivers and which they could trade. A regulation mechanism of this type could be either an alternative or a complement to congestion charging, as one of the main factors that works against the acceptability of the latter is the additional costs, or even the threat it imposes on the freedom to travel of motorists who, for whatever reason, are captive of the car.

Thus, mechanisms of this type have been devised for providing motorists with quotas of vehicle-kilometres or trips within a given urban zone, which they could then trade (Verhoef *et al.*, 1996; Marlot, 1998). An initial free allowance would provide drivers with a minimum amount of "unconstrained" travel as is the case now, while any driver travelling more than allowed for free would have to pay a price similar to a conventional congestion charge.

Such a hybrid mechanism has been analyzed from the theoretical standpoint by Daganzo (1995) for a system with untradeable quotas. Under some circumstances, this mechanism would provide a "Pareto optimal" solution, that is to say one which does not harm anybody, unlike pure congestion charging: some individuals would avoid driving on some days and drive the other days while benefiting from lower congestion, while others would prefer to buy permits to travel beyond their initial allowance. This system has been modelled on the San Francisco Bay Bridge corridor by Nakamura and Kockelman (2002) who have shown the difficulty of finding a combination of tolls and level of rationing that would benefit all user groups.

A novel "credit-based congestion pricing" mechanism has been proposed by Kockelman and Kalmanje (2005): each month, motorists would receive an allocation in the form of credits (in principle monetary), that allow them to travel on a road network or in a zone with congestion pricing. They would therefore pay nothing if they do not use up their entire allocation: beyond this, they would have to pay a congestion charge. Those who do not use up their entire allocation would be able to use their credits later or trade them in for cash. The system could be made equitable by fine tuning the initial allowance (for example, for underprivileged families). It is efficient because motorists can decide between saving credits and their travel needs. The system is neutral with regard to toll revenue, as this is entirely redistributed at the end of each month in the form of congestion credits for the following month.

This system is equivalent to rationing within the "club" of motorists, as the quotas are effectively tradable via the regulatory authority which buys back the unused quotas every month. Kara Kockelman's team at the University of Texas is continuing to study this mechanism with regard to its impacts on trip-making and property values, as well as its administrative and technical feasibility (Gulipalli *et al.*, 2005).

Raux (2008) designs in detail a similar scheme called "tradable driving rights", aiming at reducing whether trips or vehicles-kilometres, in order to control congestion, or the same target modulated on the basis of the pollutant emission categories of vehicles in order to control atmospheric pollution. An assessment is carried out on the Lyon urban area, which points at some welfare distributive issues between motorists and the community, when compared with conventional congestion charging.

Parking rights

The application of tradable permits to parking has been studied (SARECO, 2002), particularly for commuter parking in research financed by the French research programme in transport (PREDIT). The authors considered parking in terms of its direct adverse impacts (visual pollution, excessive consumption of public space on the roads, through double parking and on pavements, with the associated safety problems) and its indirect effects, due to the additional motor vehicle traffic it generates. They have examined the possibility of applying the mechanisms of the emissions permit market to it.

In a first version, a "tradable parking permit" scheme would require a closed controlled access car park exclusively reserved for a group of users who could trade permits within an institution (*i.e.* a company or a university car park). Individuals who did not use their entire allocation of daily parking rights would be able to trade them with those who wanted more by mutual consent.

Such a system within a firm would lead to market exchanges between employees, which might be biased by hierarchical relationships, ignoring the fact that the firm would have to play the role of a bank: this explains the extreme reluctance of the firms that have been contacted.

Another problem stems from the fact that (in the system that was considered) the rights were valid on any weekday. This made it impossible to predict peaks in parking demand. To avoid this problem, *i.e.* to smooth the peaks statistically, the system would have to be extended to a whole district, or even a city centre.

The authors of the study have considered a number of ways of overcoming these problems. These include a variable access "price" (a greater number of rights would be required on a day with high demand) and the need to book a parking space in advance, with the manager setting the "price" according to demand.

To sum up, while a quantity-based rationing system would seem to be feasible for closed parking (with the reservation mentioned above regarding monitoring), the idea of trading parking rights on a market seems to have been rejected (and would, furthermore, carry the risk of creating a black market). All things considered, in the current state of knowledge, pay parking and improving the monitoring of parking spaces on the public roads seem to provide the best solutions.

With regard to commuter parking, a mechanism such as the Californian "cash-out" system where the firm has to provide each employee with the choice between a free parking space or a financial reward may be of some interest (Shoup, 2005). However, this mechanism assumes that the transfer involves no additional cost for the firm (which is the case when it rents out parking spaces for their employees). It also assumes that the reward paid to the employees is not subjected to social and tax deductions.

The Alps: from the Swiss Heavy Vehicle Fee to the Alpine Crossing Exchange?

The rapid increase in road freight traffic over the Alps has prompted Switzerland to implement a number of legislative and regulatory measures which have been approved by successive referendums. A limit to the number of HGVs that could use its Alpine crossings was also added to the constitution. In the past, Switzerland imposed a 28 tonne weight limit for HGVs (compared with 40 tonnes in the European Union). Mainly as a consequence of this limit, HGV traffic has used alternative routes through Switzerland's Alpine neighbours, particularly Austria (see the section on the Ecopoint system above) and France. Due to an agreement that came into force in 2001, Switzerland undertook to increase its weight limit for HGVs progressively to 40 tonnes (this has been the case since 2005), and to construct the two new rail crossings at Loetschberg (opened in 2007) and Saint-Gothard (scheduled to open in 2017). In exchange, Switzerland introduced the Heavy Vehicle Fee. This fee is calculated on the basis of the estimated external costs of the traffic involved. The fee is levied on all HGVs without exception, and is calculated according to the number of tonne-kilometres covered in Switzerland, on the basis of the vehicle's gross weight rating (irrespective of its actual load) and Euro pollutant emissions category: since 2005, the average fee has been 2.5 Swiss centimes per tonne-kilometre[1] and will increase to a limit of 2.75 centimes after the opening of the

1. i.e. approximately €0.016.

Loetschberg tunnel. Two-thirds of the revenue from the fee goes to finance transport infrastructure.

However, these measures do not guarantee that the legally prescribed quantitative goal for traffic transfer will be achieved: in 2009 only 650,000 vehicles a year are supposed to cross the Swiss Alps by road. For this reason, a trans-Alpine Crossing Exchange ("Bourse des Passages Transalpins", BPT) and, in particular, a cap-and-trade scheme (ECOPLAN and RAPP-Trans, 2004) has been developed: a quantitative limit will be set on Alpine crossings in the form of crossing rights which will be tradable on a market.

The BPT is considered to be technically feasible, essentially because of the existence of the electronic system used for the heavy vehicle fee and the vehicle access control already operating in Alpine road tunnels: all that is required is to modify the systems at the margin to integrate transit rights. It is estimated that in 2009 a transit right will cost 200 Swiss Francs (*i.e.* approximately €127). In view of the reduction in accidents and pollution, the net effect on the overall economy is expected to be neutral.

To prevent this rationing system leading to traffic passing through neighbouring countries, the authors of the study suggest that the Alpine Crossing Exchange should be implemented in a concerted manner in all the countries involved. In addition, this type of rationing would make it necessary to modify the agreement with the European Union which prohibits capping of any sort. An international political agreement must therefore be reached before an exchange of this type is implemented.

The case of CO_2 emissions: upstream or downstream permits?

One of the first questions that arises is what should permits target – the vehicles themselves, their unit emissions, the distance they travel or their fossil fuel they consume?

The second question is the point of obligation for the permits, *i.e.* the compromise that must be reached between their effectiveness in changing behaviours (which encourages the use of a downstream point of obligation), and the minimization of implementation and operating costs (which encourages an upstream point of obligation).

The target

The targets of environmental policies have varying levels of sophistication and correspond to different extents to the theoretical ideal. From the most appropriate to the least appropriate, they are:

- the risk of climate change and its impacts on human health, which is currently a subject of controversy;
- the exposure of populations to the still uncertain impacts of climate change;
- greenhouse gas emissions, which depend on combustion processes and the intensity of the activity responsible for them: in order to target these, it would be necessary to introduce measures that apply to mobile sources, which at present seems very difficult;

- inputs in the production process for these emissions: in decreasing order of appropriateness, these are: the fuel consumed, the vehicles-kilometres travelled, and the vehicles owned.

The closer we get to the theoretical ideal, the higher the costs of measuring and monitoring effects, which in some cases become technically impossible. This is why, until now, only inputs that can be measured directly have been targeted (*i.e.* the fuel that is consumed), or economic activities that are responsible for emissions such as the vehicle-kilometres travelled, or more simply the vehicle unit emissions or even vehicle ownership.

CO_2 emissions from fossil fuels are almost proportional to the carbon content of the fuels (the conversion rate of carbon into CO_2 varies between 95 and 99.5%). It is therefore straightforward to calculate CO_2 emissions from fossil fuel consumption using a weighting coefficient that takes account of the carbon contents of petrol (2.401 kg CO_2/litre) and diesel oil (2.622 kg CO_2/litre)[2]. Permits based on fuel consumption would obey the same proportionality.

In the case of permits based on vehicle-kilometres travelled[3], the correlation with the real level of emissions is lower: for a given distance covered, real CO_2 emissions depend on vehicle class (age and compliance with EURO norms), engine capacity, the type of fuel and the style of driving (see the European MEET project).

In the case of permits that are based simply on vehicle ownership, the correlation with the real level of emissions is still lower and may even be non-existent, as the distances covered and hence the emissions for vehicles of the same type may be extremely different.

Last, if the aim is to maximize the allocative efficiency of a permit scheme, the tax base must be intersectoral and if possible uniform, *i.e.* the carbon content of the fuel. In this case, the best target for permits would be fossil fuel consumption. By applying rules of equivalence for carbon content and transformation into CO_2 between fossil motor fuels, natural gas and coal, clear rules can be drawn up for comparing the efforts made in the transport, heating and industrial sectors[4].

In short, what is recommended is the direct targeting of fuel consumption.

The choice of the point of obligation for permits

Having established that the tax base for permits should be fuel consumption, we shall now consider the point of obligation of permits, which will be at some point along the chain between the producers of fossil energy and the end users.

2. Source ADEME, France.
3. For example using counters linked to a GPS system as are being installed in HGVs.
4. Ignoring, for the time being, the emissions of other greenhouse gases, as the European Commission has done with the ETS. However, this means that the permit market must be designed at the outset to allow for the future inclusion of the other gases in the mechanism, without a complete institutional overhaul, which would be a long process with an uncertain political outcome. In addition, it must be borne in mind that the other greenhouse gases that accompany CO_2, may have potentially important impacts which are not proportional to fuel consumption. This is the case in aviation with oxides of nitrogen (NO_x) which are produced when nitrogen and oxygen in the air combine at high temperature: this may mean that multiplying factors have to be applied to CO_2 permits from the outset (see Wit *et al.*, 2005).

Several categories of players may be considered:

- the producers, importers, refiners and distributors of fossil fuels;
- motor vehicle manufacturers (for private or commercial vehicles);
- central government and local and regional authorities, as the regulators of transport taxation, transport authorities and the providers or concessionaries of transport infrastructure and services;
- trip generators (for example, shopping centres, business centres, firms and industrial estates);
- operators that provide passenger or freight transport services, motorists who provide their own transport "service".

In this context we can focus on two aspects: one, which we shall refer to as the "spatial aspect", involves the actors that influence the supply of transport infrastructure and services (local and regional authorities and operators) and the generation of demand (promoters, traffic generators); the other, which we shall refer to as the "technical focus" is only concerned with the economic acts involved in the trading of fuel between the different actors, from the importers or refiners to the final distributors.

The spatial focus

Each industrialised country (listed in Annex I of the Kyoto Protocol) is committed to complying with the Kyoto protocol and has to purchase or sell permits on the world market. The central government may decide either to pass on the price of the quotas unchanged to the different levels of local and regional government or create a domestic permit market which would be applied at the same levels, on the basis of their respective responsibilities in the area of transport. For instance Box 4 gives an overview of these responsibilities in the French institutional framework.

Box 4. The responsibilities of French public authorities in the area of transport

The 1982 Domestic Transport Policy Act (LOTI), the Air Quality Act and the Sustainable Regional Development Policy Act (amended in 1999) are essential legal instruments for defining the responsibility of the public authorities and implementing transport policies. The principal authorities concerned are the Regions, the departments and the urban agglomerations:

The Regions are responsible for organizing non-urban regional rail transport, and scheduled non-urban regional coach services. They also help to finance roads, in the framework of contracts signed between the Region and the State.

The departments are responsible for organizing non-urban bus services, school buses and local bus routes. They also maintain and improve the network of county roads.

The municipalities or groupings of municipalities are responsible for public transport in the case where an urban transport perimeter has been defined. They also have to maintain and improve the network of municipal roads (or in some cases community roads in the case of an urban community).

So, we can conceive of a system in which the permits diffuse downwards from central government to smaller and smaller regional divisions (with a stopping point to be determined).

For example, one can conceive a conceptual framework for introducing the quota concept for conurbations. The conurbations would then be free to make their residents pay for the quota scheme (see below), or use a completely different combination of regulations and pricing in order to comply with the quotas.

Using a similar approach, we could envisage controlling urban development, and indirectly the traffic it generates, by applying a building rights mechanism to property transactions (Ottensmann, 1998). This would make it necessary to identify trip generators (for example, shopping centres, small business areas and industrial estates) and raise a great many problems for organizing the market, in particular with regard to minimizing transaction costs and make trading possible within a conurbation, but perhaps also between different conurbations.

Another possibility is for the government to allocate permits to the regions, to make the latter responsible for greenhouse gas emissions in their transport policy, as proposed by Godard (2006). This allocation could be made on the basis of the region's population. A region which, as a result of investment and its transport policy in general (in particular in the areas of taxation and pricing), reduces transport emissions below its initial allocation of quotas, would be able to sell its unused quotas. Conversely, if its emissions exceed the allocated quotas, it would be liable to purchase the missing permits. Of course, this assumes that the regions, working with the departments and the urban agglomerations, are able to control emissions effectively, which is not possible with today's level of institutional fragmentation (see Box 4).

How will it be possible to measure the performance of different regional authorities for CO_2 emissions? One way would be to monitor fuel purchases within the region but, in view of the mobile nature of the sources of emissions, emissions can only be assigned to one or other region on an arbitrary basis. Another solution would be to measure traffic (VKT) in the various areas[5], and estimate emissions on the basis of vehicle unit consumptions.

However, networks are highly interlinked: a municipality that belongs to an urban community may have within its territory segments of national roads and motorways, county roads, community roads and municipal roads which drivers use one after another when they travel. Allocating emissions on a zone basis would therefore raise a number of issues. For example, if an authority such as a department improves its county roads and therefore increases the amount of road traffic travelling into another local authority such as an urban agglomeration in the same department, it is very difficult to see how it would be possible to make it bear the associated costs.

Following the idea of "city carbon budget" by Salon and Sperling (2008), local governments, which plan land use and define transport policy and hence provide transport infrastructure and services, could be involved in emission trading schemes. However, the basic difficulty is to monitor mobile sources which can be fuelled somewhere in a specific administrative area

5. This would make it necessary to intensify the collection of traffic statistics, which is only done permanently on motorways (by the concessionaries), national roads (by the Ministry of Infrastructure) and main roads in built-up areas (by the highways departments of urban communities), or in the context or cordon surveys at regular or irregular intervals of several years. The household travel surveys conducted in urban agglomerations do not generally collect actual routes, which can only be reconstituted by using traffic models.

and can travel through other administrative areas: to which local governments should the liability of emissions be attributed?

Generally speaking, the fragmentation of institutional responsibilities over different geographic areas would make it extremely complex to administer a permit scheme that would apply to regional authorities.

The technical focus

Considering the technical focus, the participants in the permit mechanism may be either upstream (*i.e.* refiners, secondary energy producers (electricity, heating) and fuel distributors), or downstream (*i.e.* final consumers such as drivers or freight and passenger transport operators).

In order to reduce administrative costs, the permit scheme should be set up far upstream, at a level where there are very few actors. A possible example is refiners or fuel distributors who have to return the product of the domestic tax on oil products to the government and are therefore accustomed to passing taxes on to the final customer. By obliging the producers and importers of oil, natural gas and coal to return the permits, the scheme would cover CO_2 emissions from the combustion of hydrocarbon fuels by all end users.

However, this benefit of universal coverage has lost some of its impact today in Europe, after the introduction of the decentralized ETS that targets energy intensive fixed facilities. An upstream permit scheme would therefore have to be adapted in order to complement the ETS.

Moreover, an upstream permit scheme suffers from two disadvantages.

The first relates to the danger of diluting the incentive provided by permits to encourage emitters to implement all the available possibilities for reducing emissions. In fact, whether the permits are purchased by auction or distributed free to fuel suppliers, the suppliers would pass on the opportunity costs[6] of these additional permits to their clients, as a simple additional charge. In this case, the advantage compared with the current system of fuel taxation is virtually non-existent.

The second disadvantage becomes apparent if fuel suppliers received a free allowance of quotas. If fuel refiners and wholesalers received a free permit allowance, what would they do with the revenue generated by it? The refiners and wholesalers could pass on the opportunity costs of their free permits: this would not threaten the economic efficiency of a system, but it certainly would endanger its acceptability, as those bearing the cost of reduction would not benefit from the revenue created by the free allocation. An upstream permit therefore seems, for reasons of political acceptability, incompatible with a free allowance[7].

These disadvantages encourage us to prefer so-called "downstream" *i.e.* decentralized permit schemes for the transport sector.

---

6. As the permits will have a value on the market, the opportunity cost for fuel suppliers would be given by not selling the permits received for free, or not recovering their value by invoicing extra costs to their consumers.

7. Unless this revenue is taxed, which is a source of additional complexity.

We shall begin by briefly describing the European Commission's proposal of including air transport via air operators, which represents a first step downstream. At the other extremity is a proposal for allocating carbon quotas to individuals that would cover all energy consumption, not just transport. The strength of this proposal lies in its comprehensiveness. However, we nevertheless consider that it is important to look in greater detail at how it might be possible to implement downstream rights allocations in the transport sector.

While the actors involved in passenger and freight transport share the target of CO_2 emissions the characteristics of competition in their respective markets differ:

• The road freight transport sector is made up of a great many very small companies, and in Europe very high intra-European and extra-European competition. Road freight transport carries 80% of domestic freight transport (in tonne-kilometres) and is in competition with rail and waterway transport, as well as air transport for express services and long-haul transport.
• Road passenger transport involves a large number of private (including households) and public actors. Households purchase and maintain private cars whose technical characteristics are defined by the manufacturers[8]. Road public passenger transport operators offering urban, suburban or interurban services work within a framework which is regulated by public service considerations and where both the services and funding are decided by the transport authorities. In the framework of the increasing liberalization of road passenger transport in Europe, these operators are also gradually coming into competition with rail and air transport, both in the case of specialized tourism services and international travel.

As a consequence, the characteristics of permit schemes for these two sectors (with regard to goals, the initial permit allowance rule, etc.), must be considered separately.

For this reason, after the two sections dealing with air transport, and carbon allocations for individuals, two separate sections will deal respectively with terrestrial passenger and terrestrial freight transport.

The inclusion of air transport in European Trading Scheme

Air traffic is undergoing very rapid growth: in Europe, for instance, growth in the number of flights has increased from 2.5 to more than 4% per year in the past 10 years and CO_2 emissions from air traffic, which rose by 73 percent between 1990 and 2003, could cancel out more than a quarter of the reduction that the European Union must achieve under the Kyoto Protocol (Wit *et al.*, 2005). According to a report issued in 1999 by the IPCC[9], aviation accounted for only a small fraction (3.5%) of anthropogenic radiative forcing en 1992, but given the pace at which air traffic is growing, this percentage is set to increase rapidly. Furthermore, the report estimates that the full impact of aviation is two to four times higher than that of its CO_2 emissions, since the nitrogen oxides it generates lead to the formation of ozone and condensation trails, whose impacts are suspected but still poorly understood[10].

8. These can be covered by unit emissions permit mechanisms, as in the ZEV programme (see above).
9. Intergovernmental Panel on Climate Change
10. For a detailed review of scientific knowledge about the physicochemical impacts of air transport emissions and a discussion of possible ways of measuring the resulting radiative forcing, see Wit *et al.*, 2005.

Although domestic air transport emissions are the responsibility of the States party to the Kyoto Protocol, the latter referred the issue of international air transport emissions to the International Civil Aviation Organization (ICAO)[11]. While the ICAO remains firmly opposed to any fuel tax on an international scale, it has agreed in principle to an emissions permit trading scheme for civil aviation as long as the system is open to other economic sectors with no distortion of market access or rights allocations.

The slow progress of negotiations at the ICAO prompted the European Commission to issue a statement in September 2005 proposing to bring aircraft operators[12] into the EU Emissions Trading System (ETS) for all flights departing from the European Union. The regime would apply to all operators, whether based in the EU or elsewhere. Based on the study it had commissioned (Wit *et al.*, 2005), the Commission considered this to be a better approach than other options[13] and that it would only have a limited impact on the price of airline tickets (between €0 and €9 per return flight within the EU). After a proposal by the Commission at the end of 2006 and a series of discussions, the European Parliament and the Council adopted a Directive at the end of 2008.

The scheme will apply to all flights (whatever the nationality of the aircraft operator) departing from or arriving at EU airports as of 2012. The total quantity of allowances will be equivalent to a fraction of historical aviation emissions (97% in 2012, 95% from 2013). These "historical aviation emissions" consist of the average CO_2 emissions for the aviation sector over the period 2004-2006. Of this total quantity of allowances, 15% will be auctioned and a special reserve will be set aside for new aircraft operators. The remaining allowances will be allocated free of charge to aircraft operators. Each operator will have to apply annually for this free allocation, based on its own historical activity (tonne-kilometres, for both freight and passengers). Unlike the current ETS scheme, the method of allocating free allowances will be harmonized across the EU. In particular, the ratio of total quantity allowances to the total number of tonne-kilometres carried by the operators will be calculated each year by the Commission. This ratio will then serve as a basis for calculating each aircraft operator's free allocation. In addition, operators will be able to buy allowances from other sectors covered by the ETS (but the opposite will not apply).

Proposals for the allocation of personal carbon quotas

Ideas about personal allocations of carbon quotas have been current for some time, and can be traced back to proposals made by David Fleming in 1996, first under the name of "Domestic Tradable Quotas (DTQ)" (Fleming, 1996) which the author then changed to "Tradable

11. The ICAO was set up in 1948 to foster the safe and ordered development of civil aviation at global level. It is a specialized agency of the United Nations and draws up the international standards and regulations that ensure the safety, security, efficiency and regularity of air transport, and is the body through which cooperation takes place between its 189 contracting states in all areas relating to civil aviation (source http://www.icao.int).

12. Which mostly, but not exclusively, consist of airlines. Non-commercial flights would therefore be included See CCE, 2005.

13. Such as taxes on air tickets, take-off and landing taxes or emissions charges.

Energy Quotas (TEQs)" (Fleming, 2006). These are energy quotas (rather than quotas for greenhouse gas emissions), which would be rationed on the basis of a dual constraint to reduce greenhouse gas emissions and maintain an equitable distribution of energy, irrespective of its source, allowing for future energy crises.

Some of these quotas would be allocated each week to adults and some would be auctioned among firms and other economic agents (including public administrations). Unused quotas could be traded on a market, with allocations, debits and sales being managed by means of chipcards on a national electronic platform. Individuals not wishing to take part in the scheme could sell their allocation of quotas immediately, but would obviously be automatically invoiced for quotas on the basis of their energy consumption.

The budget would look twenty years ahead and be established by an independent energy commission. It would be reduced regularly each week (Fleming uses the analogy of the steps of an "energy staircase" that society descends one at a time).

A scheme of this type would therefore include the entire economy of a country and cover all energy consumption within a single mechanism and market. It is obviously essential for this policy, and in particular the budget that is drawn up for the next twenty years, not to be vulnerable to changes in government.

This proposal was discussed by the United Kingdom Treasury and explicitly mentioned in the press by the British Environment Minister in July 2005.

The DTQ proposal has been subject to an initial evaluation in terms of equity, efficiency and effectiveness (Starkey and Anderson, 2005). As regards equity, an egalitarian distribution of quotas among individuals seems equitable at first sight. Nevertheless, this would have to be accompanied by the usual policies that set out to assist the poorest sections of society, who would be the first to suffer from an increase in the cost of energy. As regards effectiveness, the electronic system seems feasible (and it would appear possible to prevent fraud), while the mechanism's simplicity would make it fairly easy for the public to understand. With regard to efficiency, the authors stress that bringing 45 million persons (adults) into a system of this type may appear to be a challenge, but it would less costly than the government's proposal to set up a national identity card (with which it could be linked) or that of national road tolls. In view of its benefits in terms of equity, public acceptability and efficiency the additional cost compared with other instruments such as the carbon tax or straightforward rationing, the authors consider that a DTQ system is justified.

However, although this proposal is seductive, its application to all aspects of household energy consumption requires a comprehensive in-depth evaluation of this consumption, in particular that related to housing and transport.

Tradable fuel rights for motorists

The fact that motor vehicles represent a large number of mobile emissions sources is *a priori* a barrier to the decentralization of permit schemes in the transport sector, due to what are seen as prohibitive administrative costs. This explains why the decentralization of permits has gone no further than the level of motor manufacturers, with vehicle unit emissions as its target (see the ZEV programme described above and proposals contained in the literature: Albrecht, 2000; Wang, 1994) or household vehicle ownership (Walton, 1997). However, these schemes have the disadvantage that they ignore the other component of total emissions, namely the fuel consumption that results from actual vehicle use. The conventional view is that this consumption would be covered by an increase in existing fuel taxation, whose additional administrative and collection cost is virtually nonexistent.

Fluctuations in the price of oil mean that the efficiency of a tax is highly variable, and it is very far from having gained public acceptance (see Box 5). A CO_2 tax that aims to limit fuel consumption ought to be fixed (like the present-day French domestic tax on oil products) and not proportional to fuel price. Moreover, the amount in question should permanently change in response to fluctuations in oil price in order to ensure that consumers receive a constant price signal.

Box 5. The limits of conventional fuel taxation

The taxation instrument is widely used in the transport sector, essentially because of its tax yield. In France, fuel excise duties provided the central government with €27 billion in 2002 for a GDP of €1,522 billion. Although the current level of taxation might seem high, it is not high enough to reduce road fuel consumption. The level of additional taxation required to reduce CO2 emissions can be estimated from the price elasticity of fuel demand, whose value varies depending on whether short-term or long-term effects are taken into account. This is because, in the event of an increase in fuel price, some adaptations such as changes in driving style, reducing or optimizing some trips, or changing transport mode can be implemented in the short-term (for instance in the weeks or the months which follow the price increase). Other adaptations, such as changing one's vehicle, residential location or place of work, take longer. Price elasticity values vary between –0.3 for the short-term[14] and –0.7 for the long-term (Goodwin, 1988). This is ordinary elasticity, related to a Marshallian (or non-compensated) demand function, which therefore includes substitution and income effects.

We can obtain some orders of magnitude for the case of France. As a result of a large increase in the price of crude, the price paid by the consumer for premium grade petrol increased by 17% (from €0.9 to €1.06) between February 1999 and February 2000. In view of the short-term elasticity, fuel consumption and traffic should have been affected immediately. However, both parameters continued to rise in 1999 and only stabilized in 2000 before rising again in 2001 (URF, 2003). This is no doubt due to the sustained economic growth that occurred at the end of the 1990s. The amount of tax required to reduce GHG emissions should also therefore take account of the income elasticity of fuel demand, which is positive. In other terms, in order to remain effective, the tax on greenhouse gases should increase at the same rate as the economy grows.

Furthermore, variations in the price of petrol are likely to cancel out the effect of the tax on the end consumer. The turnaround in the oil market that took place in 2001 essentially cancelled out the 1999-2000 price rise, as the price of premium grade unleaded petrol returned to a little under €1 (the usual level in 2002 and 2003): the price effects of a CO_2 tax would have been wiped out.

Last, the "tax rebellion" that took place in several European countries in September 2000 shows how sensitive public opinion is to fuel taxation (Lyons and Chatterjee, 2002). Central government is a focus for opposition as it benefits from the tax, although it has little control over oil prices.

14. i.e. if the fuel price increases by 10%, fuel demand falls by 3%.

The examples of the Austrian Ecopoints system which operated for a number of years (see above), electronic road tolling for HGVs in Germany, which has been in operation since 2005, or the Transalpine Crossing Exchange project (see above), show that monitoring the transactions performed by a large number of mobile sources does not involve any insurmountable technical and economic difficulties.

Decentralization of the permit system in the transport sector has some benefits in that transaction costs would be largely offset by the benefits in terms of efficiency, acceptability and equity arising from permit schemes.

A CO_2 emissions permit scheme that applies to fuel consumption by motorists has been proposed by Raux and Marlot (2001, 2005), on the grounds that private cars account for approximately three-fifths of fuel sales, the rest being consumed by light commercial vehicles and HGVs. We present the main features of this proposal below.

Target and allocation

With regard to effectiveness, the ideal situation would be to operate at the most decentralized level possible. The permit should therefore be associated with a litre of fuel. Its value could be varied according to the type of fuel, on the basis of the average amount of CO_2 emitted by its combustion (diesel oil contains more carbon than petrol). For the sake of simplicity, in this presentation, we shall assume that the permit unit is linked to a litre of fuel.

Free allocation of permits minimizes problems of social and political acceptability as it would allow a certain amount of fuel to be consumed without incurring any additional cost. This would mean a minimum amount of travel could be guaranteed to users who possess no viable alternative to the car.

For example, we could take as our starting point an average consumption rounded to 1,000 litres per car per year[15]. If we imposed a 10% reduction in this consumption, 900 permits (900 litres) would have to be allocated per car.

In order to consume more than 900 litres, a consumer would have to purchase additional permits on the market. On the other hand, consumers who do not use all the permits they have been given could sell them. The possibility of selling permits would provide an additional incentive for modifying behaviours, particularly for individuals who can do so at low cost. The permits would have unlimited validity[16].

The sale and purchase of permits would be supervised at national level by a regulatory authority. The permits awarded annually would be held on a chipcard which records permit debit and credit operations. This card would be compatible with the Automatic Teller Machines (ATM) that are already installed at petrol stations. Permits would therefore be debited or purchased at the rate that applies when the fuel is purchased. Permits could also be pur-

15. Our quantitative simulations were performed for 1997, which was the most recent year for which data on the car fleet and fuel consumption were available in France (the SOFRES-ADEME Parc Auto panel, see Hivert, 1999). Based on the mileages and unit consumption figures which were reported by the panel (13,719 km on average, and slightly less than 7.5 l/100 km), average annual consumption was 1,022 litres.

16. which might lead to hoarding and speculation.

chased or resold in banks, using ATM bank distributors, or on the Internet. In view of the large number of actors involved, the exchange would not be bilateral but rather centralized in an exchange market which would publish the daily value of the permit.

A combined taxation and permit system

It would be socially unacceptable to make the transition suddenly from a tax-based system to a permit-based system. Moreover, participation in the permit scheme should be voluntary. The two systems would therefore have to coexist, with the creation of a financial incentive for joining the permit system.

Also, in order to reduce administrative costs, permit utilization operations would have to be validated as near as possible to the time of fuel purchase, that is to say when the motorist buys fuel at the pump. It would therefore not be possible to create an impenetrable administrative barrier between the system of taxation and the system of permits.

The solution would be to set up a single tax *t* (referred to as the "CO_2 tax"), which would be paid both by fuel consumers outside the permit market and those who take part in it but who have used up their allocation and who are either unable or unwilling to purchase permits on the market. This tax would therefore limit rises in the price of permits on the market, constituting a "maximum price".

Towards an appraisal

In view of the fact that the transactions and verifications required for the permits would be highly integrated with the current system of bank card transactions, (it would simply be necessary to alter the software in the ATM at petrol stations and install the microcode software on existing bank chipcards during periodic replacement) the implementation and administrative costs should be moderate.

The surpluses that have been calculated with a variety of hypotheses regarding elasticities and according to household residential location (city centre, suburbs, peri-urban and rural)[17] provide two areas for debate:

- the first relates to the choice between taxation and permits and is illustrated by the scale of the fiscal gain in the case of the tax and the fiscal loss for central government in the case of permits[18]. Nevertheless, this loss would only represent approximately 5% of current fiscal revenue from fuel consumption.
- the second relates to the distribution of surpluses between households according to their location. In the case of taxation, this would have little effect on the tax levy which is already high: all motorists would "lose" to the benefit of the community. However, in the case of permits, the above tax levy would disappear and residential location would play a fundamental role: the winners would be those households living in the city centre or the suburbs who,

17. The methodological details and fuller results were published in Raux and Marlot (2005). The quantitative exercise was performed with 1997 consumption data and fuel prices.
18. Permits would be traded between actors and reductions in fuel consumption would lead to equivalent reductions in fiscal revenue from present-day taxation.

on average, would sell permits (it is easier for them to reduce their vehicle-kilometres travelled) while the households living in peri-urban areas would on average be the largest purchasers.

This system would have the advantage of simplicity, as the unit of exchange is the permit for each litre of fuel consumed. The amounts consumed or exchanged would therefore be monitored when fuel is purchased, and all persons purchasing fuel would be able to participate in the market (see below for the case of commercial vehicles): monitoring would therefore be straightforward as it only involves fuel purchases, and there would be no need to measure actual emissions. The existence of an upper bound on permit prices due to the CO_2 tax and the possibility of trading permits would counteract any tendency for a black market to develop.

This system would penalize high income households more than others: French data from 1997 show that average annual mileage for each car increases fairly steadily with income, from slightly more than 12,000 km for the lowest income brackets (less than €11,500 per annum) to almost 16,000 km for the highest income brackets (more than €60,000 per annum).

Likewise, the initial free allocation would avoid placing an excessive burden on consumers, particularly the least well off. The average annual consumption of cars varies from slightly more than 900 litres (for the lowest incomes) to 1,300 or 1,400 litres (for the highest incomes), while the proportion of mileage that is covered on home-to-work trips varies between 24% (for the lowest incomes) and 30 or even 39% for the highest income groups. These figures show that "necessary" travel would generally not be affected. However, this average data should not obscure a possible existence of situations of fragility, for example the "rural poor" who have no alternative but the car; such situations would require *ad hoc* compensation.

The free allocation is linked to an act of economic consumption (car ownership and use) which would moderate the windfall effect caused by the fact that permits are free. The incentive to increase the number of cars one owns would be limited by vehicle maintenance costs (periodic vehicle inspections). The windfall effect could only come into play if the price of permits on the markets became very high: however, it would be limited by the CO_2 tax.

A free allocation to motorists may mean that those without a car would feel unfairly treated. Other allocation rules can be considered on the grounds of equity: the allocation could be individual (as described above in the case of DTQs). Equity issues may also be raised if everybody receives the same allocation, as some groups are affected by specific constraints, *i.e.* the disabled or those living in the country, etc. There is no reason why the allocation method should not take account of these factors.

The domestic nature of the permit market would appear to be viable in view of the generally short distances involved in car trips and if we ignore the impact of "tank tourism" at borders, which is a problem that has already been encountered with taxation. But this closure of the market could only be temporary. The transport sector permit market could be open or closed to the national or international permit market, depending on whether or not the public authorities wish to protect the sector from permit price fluctuations on the international market, for various social or political reasons. If permit allocation was too limited or too generous, or if the CO_2 tax (the maximum permit price) was not at the correct level, the marginal costs of reducing CO_2 would not be the same in different sectors. Such distortions would reduce the efficiency of the system. They can therefore only be envisaged as transitional measures before the introduction of a market which will ultimately be open.

This system would provide strong incentives for reducing consumption because of the concrete and tangible benefits received by those who reduce their emissions below their initial allocation. The free allocation of permits would furthermore provide a means of overcoming the problems of accessibility and equity which would be posed by the addition of a new tax on an already heavily taxed product such as fuel.

Fuel consumption permits for freight transport

After our consideration of research into emission permits for motorists, we shall turn to other research on "downstream" permits involving freight transport[19].

The answers with regard to the definition of the quantitative target, *i.e.* the nature of the quota, are similar to those obtained in the previous case. However, the nature of freight transport means we must apply a different approach to deciding which entities should hold the quotas. Below, we shall discuss the issue of whether the quota allowances should be free or not, and if not, what allocation method should be used. We will then define the geographical and sectoral coverage of the permit scheme before going on to consider monitoring and management. Last, we will assess the possible environmental and economic impacts of a scheme of this type.

The target

As we have seen above, on the grounds of environmental effectiveness the target should be as near as possible to CO_2 emissions, and therefore fossil fuel consumption. The tradable quotas would thus be CO_2 quotas calculated on the basis of the carbon content of the fuel consumed by the transport undertaking during the transport operation. The transport undertaking would have to return quotas to the regulator for the fossil fuel it purchases (and therefore subsequently burns). This system would apply to all those using transport vehicles, *i.e.* public hauliers and shippers using own-account transport.

Taking account of the large number of actors and decisions

Which entities would hold, trade and return the permits for the emissions that are generated? And, consequently, which actors would have to pay for the permits?

The fact that fuel consumption is targeted naturally means the incentives apply to the hauliers. However, the way the logistical chain operates at present leaves them with very small margins for manœuvre. Shippers' requirements in terms of frequencies, deadlines and services impose conditions on the hauliers. Could actors that are further upstream in the logistical

19. This research is currently being conducted by the LET as part of the PREDIT programme and has been financed by the ADEME.

chain be brought into the permit scheme to guarantee the efficiency of the incentives, and in what ways?

This issue arises from the fact that transport activity and its resulting greenhouse gas emissions are the outcome of a set of decisions taken by actors whose economic strategies sometimes diverge.

We can identify four levels of decision-making, from the most strategic level, that of decisions regarding the industrial and geographical structure of the firm's production and distribution (1), then the scheduling of this production and distribution (2), followed by the organization of transport (3), and last the performance of transport itself (4). Decisions regarding level 1 have consequences on the volume of traffic of both intermediate and final goods (tonnages and distances, *i.e.* ultimately tonne-kilometres). Decisions with regard to level 2 (requirements concerning the scheduling of consignments) and level 3 (the organization of transport in response to these requirements) have impacts on vehicle-kilometres travelled per transport mode, as well as filling rates and empty runs. Last, decisions with regard to level 4 (choice of motor vehicle and driving style) have impacts on the nominal and real unit consumptions of vehicles.

These different levels of decision-making may be controlled by a wide variety of actors. In general, a firm producing goods will cover at least levels 1 and 2 although level 2 is sometimes controlled by orders downstream, perhaps through a logistical service provider. The firm may either limit its involvement to levels 1 and 2 or go as far as level 3 by organizing its own logistics then using third-party transport (level 4), or alternatively cover part or all of level 4 (using own-account transport). A specialized transport undertaking will cover at least level 4, often level 3 and may, *via* logistical services, go as far back as level 2.

The ability of tradable permits to minimize the total cost of reducing emissions applies in an ideal world without transaction costs. However, in reality, there is a large number of actors with unequal powers of negotiation, all of which make decisions.

For a firm using own-account transport (*i.e.* one that covers levels 1 to 4), the problem does not seem insurmountable: we can imagine how, with a given initial allowance (see below) and the obligation to return quotas to the regulator in proportion to its motor fuel purchases, the firm would optimize its activities, if necessary purchasing quotas on the market.

In the case of third-party transport, the question is more complex, in view of the current dependency of hauliers on the shippers. We therefore need to create a system which would allow the reduction efforts to be distributed between shippers and hauliers, taking account of their respective margins for manœuvre.

To sum up, a system would be applied to all firms irrespective of the nature of their activities, along the same lines as the European Directive on quotas. Firms using third-party transport and transport operators would be covered by a quota monitoring mechanism to be specified as follows.

What about quota transfers between hauliers and shippers? Our surveys have shown that, as a consequence of fuel price rises, the use of contractual indexing or the added charge to invoice total seem to be fairly widespread practices, in spite of the disapproval of some shippers. The practice has been formalized in France by a 2006 act which introduced the fuel charges explicitly in the basis of payment for transport operations. This law also introduced an obligation to revise the price of the transport service to take account of variations in these charges. In all cases, the invoice must show the fuel charges that have been met in order to perform the transport service.

Quota transfer using the added charge to invoice total therefore seems possible. It would provide a way of giving the haulier some security with respect to the implementation of fuel quotas. In the same way that today invoices should show fuel charges, in the future they could show the number of quotas used[20] to carry out the transport operation.

A free allowance or none?

There are two possible types of initial allowance, one that is sold or one that is provided free. The first has the advantage of avoiding complex calculations of allowances, which require data which is sometimes expensive to collect. It also avoids involving the authorities in hard negotiations with the agents targeted by the permit scheme, leaving the market to decide. For proof of this, we need look no further than the intense negotiation that took place in Germany and France between the government and the firms producing large amounts of CO_2 in the framework of the initial application of the ETS in 2004-2005.

However, the sale of permits is very likely to be seen as an additional tax, which would reduce their acceptability. It is for this reason that proposals involving free allowances have been examined.

The main issue in connection with free allowances is equity for the different actors. Their perception of this will determine how acceptable they find the method. This is why several permit allocation methods have been developed successively and then evaluated. For example, an allowance which is applied only to hauliers would in no way change the balance of power between hauliers and shippers, with the danger that the latter would make the former bear most of the cost of emissions reduction. It is therefore important to consider how permits could be allocated to shippers in order to include them explicitly in the process.

The allocation methods which have been tested in the course of in-depth interviews with about twenty firms, half of them shippers and half carriers, have raised a large number of issues. The reporting of data from shippers about fuel consumption and vehicle-kilometres travelled seems to be a particularly difficult area: the envisaged audits would therefore be particularly costly (even if they were restricted to those firms who volunteered to take part in the system). An allocation norm based on an average quota ratio per tonne-kilometre, even if it was personalized for each shipper, seemed unjustified and was contested. The declarative nature of this information and the fact that value is created by the allocation mechanism would make fraudulent behaviour extremely likely and, even if it remained rare, this would undermine the mechanism's credibility. Overall, these shortcomings[21] and the complexity of the allocation mechanisms were responsible for reluctance or even opposition on the part of most of the shippers we interviewed.

20. On the basis of the carrier's estimation of average CO_2 emissions per tonne-kilometre. This involves for the carrier monitoring accurately its fuel consumption.
21. Without forgetting the known shortcomings of this type of "grandfathering" allocation.

As a result of these difficulties, we recommend abandoning any free allocation method, at least for the shippers, in favour of the sale of quotas by the regulator. However, a free allocation could be devised for transport operators in order to improve the acceptability of the scheme, *e.g.* a "lump sum" allocation per vehicle for road hauliers. Given the European scale, the principle of a free allocation or not and, if a free allocation is adopted, the choice of the method of allocation and the calculation of the allocations would be decided on the level of the European Union.

Sectoral and geographical coverage

A market of this type for freight transport would have to cover at least the entire European Union, for obvious reasons to do with harmonization and competition between firms in different countries. This would mean, in particular, that if the principle of a free allowance was adopted in spite of everything, the allocation and calculation method would have to be decided at European Union level.

On the grounds of environmental efficiency it would be necessary to cover all the modes that use fossil fuel, *i.e.* road, rail, waterways, maritime and air transport. It would also make it necessary to cover other sectors of transport, in particular private cars (see above), either by a permit market or by a CO_2 taxation mechanism.

European Union scale geographical coverage would make it possible to include all the intra-European international links, in particular air and maritime links. Despite international and maritime transport are not covered by the Kyoto protocol, air travel in the European Union will be soon included in the ETS (see above) while the case of maritime transport is pending.

In order to facilitate the transition towards the quota scheme, this would have to co-exist with a conventional taxation system. Firms and carriers would join a quota scheme on a voluntary basis. A so-called "commercial" fuel (petrol or diesel) which would have a lower level of excise duty[22], would be reserved to businesses taking part in the quota scheme. The users of road freight transport vehicles who decide not to take part in a quota scheme would pay the standard "CO_2 tax" on the fuel they use[23].

Monitoring and management, transaction costs

The efficiency of the system would depend on the ability to monitor emissions and manage the permit market without transaction costs becoming prohibitive.

We have already seen that the free allocation methods we have analyzed would involve large data collection costs and the risk of fraudulent use of the system, which were partly responsible for their rejection. Removing the free allocation option would do away with the costs of data collection and combating fraud.

With respect to transactions, quota transfers between shippers and carriers would be covered by their contractual arrangements, as is now the case for transport services. These contractual

22. Similar to the "commercial diesel oil" whose introduction was envisaged in the Draft Directive COM (2002) 410 on fuel taxation, which was rejected by the European Parliament in December 2003.
23. Which would correspond to the full discharge penalty for insufficient quotas (see above).

relationships are already subject to legislative and regulatory measures, without any need for authorities to intrude in the relationships so no additional administrative costs would be incurred. Likewise, trading on the permit market would not be bilateral but would pass through a central exchange: finding a partner for trading would therefore involve no costs.

Monitoring and control would therefore only involve the transfer of quotas to a regulator at the time of fuel purchase. Road fuel is either purchased at a pump, or from a tank on company's site. In the case of purchase at a fuel station, in particular one reserved for HGVs, the driver in most cases uses a magnetic card or a smartcard. The software on these cards and the fuel feeds would have to be changed in order to debit quotas according to the amount of fuel which is purchased. The participation of a transport company in the quota market would oblige it to use this type of card exclusively when purchasing fuel at the fuel station. When a transport company fills its onsite tank, the fuel supplier's invoice would include the debit of quotas from the transport company account (or these quotas would be invoiced in the case of a transport company that does not take part in the permit market). Ultimately, the risk of fraud is rather small.

What would be the risk of players abusing their dominant position on the permit market? Would some players have so much market power that they could distort competition and the price mechanisms on the permit market? We think the danger of this is negligible: in the transport sector, the number of players and the dispersion of transport demand between them is such that it is unlikely that any single actor would have sufficient power[24].

The sectoral and geographical coverage and the mechanism that are envisaged allow us to state that the CO_2 quota market would not discriminate against shippers or carriers from any of the 27 Member States of the European Union.

One legitimate question remains, that of possible competition from carriers from outside the European Union. However, freight transport is less subject to economic relocations than other sectors of activity: freight must always be loaded at fixed locations in order to be carried for use at other fixed locations, whether what is involved is the factories where final products are manufactured or the sites where they are delivered or sold. Insofar as cabotage by carriers from outside the European Union is limited, the only marked effect would be due to carriers buying fuel with a low level of tax outside the borders of the European Union, in order to transport goods on a journey with an intra-European leg. Such competition might have some importance in border countries, but it would be limited by the trade-off that would have to be made between the weight of fuel involved and the payload.

24. For example, Arcelor, which is the largest shipper in Europe handles less than 1% of the tonne-kilometres transported in France (information provided personally).

Conclusion

Monitoring a large number of mobile sources presents no major technical problem

It is technically possible to construct a system in which permits are associated with mobile sources with acceptable financial costs in order to protect the local environment of sensitive regions, as has been shown by the Ecopoint programme in Austria. From the technical point of view, this system requires the installation of simple equipment in the vehicles and electronic detection gantries at the points of entry to the zone to be protected. An examination of the limitations of the Ecopoint programme has shown that in order to provide full coverage of vehicles, the region to be protected must have a small number of entry or passage points that are easy to observe. The Swiss project for an Alpine Crossing Exchange obviously represents an effective compromise for limiting the increase in road freight transport in the Alpine region.

Likewise, in the last twenty years, technical advances in on-board electronics have made it possible to introduce electronic tolling systems. This means it is quite conceivable to introduce credit-based congestion pricing schemes, which make the regulation of road congestion by price in urban areas more efficient, more equitable and therefore more acceptable.

Permit markets operating between automobile manufacturers are viable

A system of credits linked to unit vehicle emissions which can be traded between manufacturers is quite feasible, as has been shown by the Californian ZEV programme, even though it is not yet fully mature: the additional administrative costs are negligible compared with the normal administrative costs of monitoring and applying regulations.

On the other hand, the early failure of the voluntary agreement between motor manufacturers selling light vehicles in Europe highlights the benefits that would be associated with such systems for vehicle fleet marketed in Europe.

The keys to the success of such programmes are clarity, simplicity and pragmatism

The successes and failures of cases where permit markets have been implemented for managing natural resources and pollution are particularly instructive.

The criteria of clarity, simplicity and pragmatism are important for the success of tradable permit schemes. Clarity demands that the nature of the quota which is traded or banked must be unambiguous. Simplicity concerns the rules for managing transfers which must be as easy as possible, in order to take advantage of the benefits of the tradable nature of permits. Last, the design of the scheme must be pragmatic in order to be able to change in various ways in response to disparities between the goals and our developing understanding of the cost borne by the participants in the programme.

The fact that these criteria were applied explains the success of the lead phasedown programme in the United States, due to the straightforward definition of the permit unit (a gram of lead), simple rules and a high degree of freedom in trading as well as pragmatism in the way the programme and its various options were implemented.

The failure to comply with these criteria on the other hand explains the failures that have occurred, both for some markets for the right to draw water and others relating to water pollution: these failures can be put down to the fact that in some cases several players can oppose the transactions, and in other cases actors who buy permits have to prove they need them and transactions are subject to the approval of the authorities.

Clarity also contributed to the success of the Ecopoints programme in Austria and the ZEV programme in California. In both cases the tax base was clearly stated (respectively grams NOx per kWh and grams of NMOG per mile).

Likewise, in the ZEV programme, the regulatory authority is not involved in trading between the programme participants[1], and such simplicity facilitates the implementation of this type of programme. The ZEV programme also provides good examples of pragmatism: changes in the types of credit during the scheme development make it easier for motor manufacturers to adapt.

However, pragmatism seems to have been lacking from the Ecopoints system. If a programme of this type were to be applied at European Union level, the agreement of all Member States would be needed before any modification. It is easy to imagine the difficulties this would pose in view of the diverging interests of the different countries.

This highlights the fact that pragmatism is only possible if the regulatory authority has strong political support and far-reaching powers.

Political will and public support are essential

A regulatory authority often needs to negotiate with professional groups that can apply strong political pressure. To be able to do so it must have real power, that reflects the political will.

The smaller the possibilities of adaptation at low cost the stronger the political will that is required. The lead phasedown programme provides an example of the opposite situation, where affordable alternative solutions were available

Our examination of the ZEV programme has shown that the dynamic equilibrium between political will and opposing pressure from motor manufacturers has always played a role in

1. There were no transfers in the Ecopoints programme because it was not designed for this.

the programme's development and continues to do so. The 1996 reform which pushed back the 1998 deadline for the ZEV mandate to 2003 and introduced a voluntary agreement, was seen by many as a victory for the motor manufacturers, whose arguments concerning the jobs provided by the industry had particular political resonance. However, environmental pressure groups, supported by strong public awareness of local air pollution, played an important role in the public debate surrounding the programme, and in the CARB's confirmation of the ZEV programmes goals.

However, it is not certain that the political will exists for limiting greenhouse gas emissions from transport, or if it does that it is strong enough compared with the scale of the necessary changes. It cannot be said that public opinion is not gradually becoming aware of the seriousness of the problem. However, the fact that the effects on the global climate will occur in the distant future and involve a degree of uncertainty combine with what is considered to be the unacceptable social cost of the lifestyle changes that are required immediately, leading to delay in taking the necessary decisions.

What role can tradable permits play in the reduction of greenhouse gas emissions from transport?

The terms of this debate are familiar. We cannot count on the technological advances that are anticipated in the medium term to meet our CO_2 emissions reductions targets, which means we must modify vehicle use. The possible ways of reducing demand are taxation, permits or a combination of the two. In view of the fact that fuel taxation already exists, extending it in the form of a "CO_2 tax" would be less expensive to administer than a permit scheme for a large number of mobile sources of pollution.

The "tax rebellion" that took place in a number of European countries in 2000, when a rise in the oil price increased the fuel price which is already highly taxed, highlights the fact that significant additional increases in fuel taxation would be unacceptable.

This is why we have proposed a number of downstream decentralization approaches for the transport sector as a possible alternative to simply increasing fuel taxation. Such hybrid approaches combining permits and a "maximum price" would make it possible to take advantage of the certainty the quantitative limit will be achieved, the additional incentive for the consumer of being able to sell unused permits, and limited permit price increase. Last, striking advances in communication and data processing technology (*i.e.* smartcards and the Internet) mean that administrative costs could be kept at a reasonable level.

An objection relates to the need for international coordination between countries. Indeed, taxation is an area in the EU legislation where unanimity is required from Member States (which are 27 today). While some countries support the idea of a carbon tax (some of them like Sweden or Finland have already implemented such a tax), others are fiercely opposed to any greater cooperation on energy taxation issue, which they see as an interference in their own domestic taxation policy. On the contrary, in the EU legislation procedures, emissions trading comes under environmental matter and there is no need for unanimity but rather for "qualified majority" voting, that is to say a majority of countries suffices to impose such a legislation.

Recently in June 2010 a new proposal for a European carbon tax was dismissed again by the European Commission. These 20 years of political discussion about carbon taxation in Europe without any step forward are to be opposed to the speed of ETS implementation: the Green Paper on GHG emissions trading within the European Union was issued in 2000 and the Directive on ETS in 2003 with an entry in force in 2005.

Another objection raises the extremely difficult issue of the implementation of what would be perceived as a form of rationing of travel. However, the acceptability of rationing is an issue in the case of both taxation and quotas: at the very least, a major information campaign and strong sustained political will would be required.

Last, the proposals presented above do not claim to represent the only possibilities available for the practical implementation of permit markets. Of course, some problems still remain to be solved, but we feel that we have shown that the potential benefits are sufficient to justify a deeper analysis of the technical, institutional and economic feasibility of schemes of this type.

However, the need for further analysis must not be used as an excuse for delay. The technological and economic changes that are needed to move towards the deep cuts in GHG emissions by 2050 are long-term processes, which means we must act now.

Bibliography

Alberola E. Prix des quotas de CO_2: premiers enseignements. *Lettre trimestrielle de la Mission Climat de la Caisse des Dépôts* 2006; (5).

Albrecht J. The diffusion of cleaner vehicles in CO_2 emission trading designs. *Transportation Research Part D.* 2000; 5: 385-401.

Baumol W & Oates W. *The Theory of Environmental Policy.* Cambridge: Cambridge University Press, 1988.

CARB. *Staff Report. 2000 Zero Emission Vehicle Program Biennial Review.* California Air Resources Board, Sacramento, 2000a.

CARB. *Secondary Benefits of the Zero-Emission Vehicle Program.* Research Division. California Air Resources Board, Sacramento, 2000b.

CARB. *Staff Report. Initial Statements of Reasons.* California Air Resources Board, Sacramento, 2001.

CCE. *Réduction de l'impact de l'aviation sur le changement climatique.* Bruxelles: Commission des Communautés Européennes, COM (2005), 459 final, 2005, 15 p.

CEC. *Report from the Commission to the Council on the Transit of Goods by Road through Austria.* Brussels: Commission of the European Communities, COM (2000), 862 final, December 2000, 30 p. + annexes.

Chin A, Smith P. Automobile Ownership and Government Policy: The Economics of Singapore's Vehicle Quota Scheme. *Transportation Research Part A* 1997; 31: 129-40.

CITEPA. <http://www.citepa.org>, mai 2006.

Coase R. The problem of Social Cost. *Journal of Law and Economics*1960; 3: 1-44.

Crals E, Vereeck L. Taxes, Tradable Rights and Transaction Costs. *European Journal of Law and Economics* 2005; 20: 199-223.

Daganzo CF. A Pareto Optimum Congestion Reduction Scheme. *Transportation Research B* 1995; 29: 139-54.

Dales JH. Land, water and ownership. *Canadian Journal of Economics* 1968; 1: 797-804.

EC. *Reducing CO2 emissions from light-duty vehicles.* <http://ec.europa.eu/environment/air/transport/co2/co2_home.htm>, April 2009.

ECOPLAN, RAPP-Trans. *Alpentransitbörse (La bourse des passages transalpins).* Berne: Ecoplan, 2004, 145 p.

ENERDATA, LEPII. Étude pour une prospective énergétique concernant la France. Rapport pour la DGEMP, Paris, 2005.

Euractiv. EU *Emissions Trading Scheme.* <http://www.euractiv.com/en/climate-change/eu-emissions-trading-scheme/article-133629>, April 2009.

Fleming D. Stopping the traffic. *Country Life*1996; 140 (19): 62-5.

Fleming D. *Energy and the Common Purpose. Descending the Energy Staircase with Tradable Energy Quotas (TEQs).* <www.teqs.net>, 2006.

Foster V, Hahn R. Designing more efficient markets: lessons from Los Angeles Smog Control. *Journal of Law and Economics* 1995; 38: 19-48.

Friedman D, Wright J, Sperling D, Burke A, Moore R. *Partial ZEV Credits. An Analysis of the California Air Resources Board LEV II Proposal to Allow Non-ZEV's to Earn Credit Toward the 10% ZEV Requirement of 2003.* Institute of Transport Studies, University of California, Davis, 1998.

Godard O. L'expérience américaine des permis négociables. *Économie Internationale* 2000; 82: 13-43.

Godard O. *Une évaluation du plan national français d'affectation des quotas d'émission de* CO_2. Communication au Séminaire sur les marchés de droits pour la gestion des problèmes environnementaux, Montpellier, 20-22 octobre 2004.

Godard O. La pensée économique face à l'environnement. In: Leroux A, Livet P. (dir). *Leçons de philosophie économique, Volume 2: Économie normative et philosophie morale.*Paris: Economica, 2005.

Godard O. *Transports et développement durable : les conditions de la compatibilité.* Cahier n° DDX-06-17, Chaire de développement durable, École Polytechnique, Paris, 2006, 21 p.

Godard O, Henry C. Les instruments des politiques internationales de l'environnement : la prévention du risque climatique et les mécanismes de permis négociables. In: Conseil d'Analyse Économique auprès du Premier Ministre. *Fiscalité de l'environnement.* Paris: La Documentation Française, Collection des Rapports du CAE, juillet 1998, 83-174.

Goodwin PB. *Evidence on car and public transport demand elasticities 1980-1988*, TSU Ref 427, Oxford, June 1988.

Greene DL. CAFE or PRICE? An analysis of the effects of federal fuel economy regulations and gasoline price on new car mpg. *The Energy Journal* 1990; 11: 1978-89.

Gulipalli P, Kalmanje S, Kockelman KM. *Credit-Based Congestion Pricing: Expert Expectations and Guidelines for Application*. Proceedings of the 84th Annual Meeting of the Transportation Research Board, 2005.

Hahn R, Hester G. Marketable permits: lessons for theory and practice. *Ecology Law Quarterly* 1989; 16: 361-406.

Hivert L. *Le parc automobile des ménages. Étude en fin d'année 1997*. Rapport de convention INRETS-ADEME. Arcueil: INRETS, juin 1999, 151 p.

IEEP. Service contract to carry out economic analysis and business impact assessment of CO2 emissions reduction measures in the automotive sector. Brussels: Institute for European Environmental Policy, June 2005, 123 p.

Jancovici JM. *L'avenir climatique. Quel temps ferons nous?* Paris: Le Seuil, Collection Science ouverte, 2002.

Kaysi I, Mahmassani H, Arnaout S, Kattan L. Phasing out lead in automotive fuels: conversion considerations, policy formulation, and application to Lebanon. *Transportation Research Part D* 2000; 403-18.

Kerr S, Maré D. *Transaction Costs and Tradable Permit Markets: The United States Lead Phase-down*. Working Paper, Motu Economic Research, Wellington, 1998.

Kerr S, Newell R. *Policy-Induced Technology Adoption: Evidence from the US Lead Phase-down*. Discussion Paper 01-14, Resources for the Future, Washington, 2001.

Kockelman KM, Kalmanje S. Credit-Based Congestion Pricing: A Proposed Policy and the Public's Response. *Transportation Research 39A* 2005: 671-90.

Koh WTH, Lee DCK. The vehicle quota system in Singapore: an assessment. *Transportation Research Part A* 1994; 28: 31-47.

Le Treut H, Jancovici JM. *L'effet de serre. Allons-nous changer le climat?* Paris: Flammarion, Collection Dominos, 2001.

Lewis J. *Lead Poisoning: A Historical Perspective*. EPA Journal, US EPA History Office, 1985.

Lyons A, Chatterjee K. (eds). *Transport Lessons from the Fuel Tax Protests of 2000*. Ashgate: Aldershot, 2002.

Marlot G. *Réguler la congestion par des permis négociables: une solution au dilemme efficacité/acceptabilité*. 8th WCTR, Antwerp, 1998.

Montgomery WD. Markets and licenses and efficient pollution control programs. *Journal of Economic Theory* 1972; 5: 395-418.

MTETM/SESP. *Les comptes des transports en 2005* (tome 1). 2006.

Nakamura K, Kockelman KM. Congestion pricing and road space rationing: an application to the San Francisco Bay Bridge corridor. *Transportation Research Part A* 2002; 36: 403-17.

Nussbaum BD. Phasing down lead in gasoline in the US: mandates, incentives, trading and banking. In Jones T, Corfee-Morlot J. (eds). *Climate Change: Designing a Tradable Permit System*. Paris: Organisation for Economic Cooperation and Development, 1992.

OECD. *Putting Markets to Work. The Design and Use of Marketable Permits and Obligations*. Paris: Organisation for Economic Cooperation and Development, Public Management Occasional Paper 19, 1997.

OECD. *Lessons from Existing Trading Systems for International Greenhouse Gas Emissions Trading*. Paris: Organisation for Economic Cooperation and Development, Environment Directorate, 1998.

OECD. *Domestic Transferable Permits for Environmental Management. Design and Implementation*. Paris: Organisation for Economic Cooperation and Development, 2001.

OECD. *Cutting Transport CO_2 Emissions. What Progress?* Paris: Organisation for Economic Cooperation and Development-ECMT, 2001.

Ottensmann JR. Market-based exchanges of rights within a system of performance zoning. *Planning and Markets* 1998; 1.

Radanne P. *La division par 4 des émissions de dioxyde de carbone en France d'ici 2050*. Rapport de mission. Mission Interministérielle de l'Effet de Serre, Paris, 2004, 32 p.

Raux C. The use of transferable permits in the transport sector. In OECD (ed). *Implementing Domestic Tradable Permits. Recent Developments and Future Challenges*. Paris: Organisation for Economic Cooperation and Development, 2002.

Raux C. The use of transferable permits in transport policy. *Transportation Research Part D* 2004; 9/3: 185-97.

Raux C. Tradable Driving Rights in Urban Areas: Their Potential for Tackling Congestion and Traffic-Related Pollution. In: Ison S, Rye T. (eds). *The Implementation and Effectiveness of Transport Demand Management Measures*. Ashgate: Aldershot, 2008, 95-120.

Raux C. Downstream Emissions Trading for Transport. In: Rotthengatter W, Hayashi Y, Schade W. (eds). *Transport Moving to Climate Intelligence: New Chances for Controlling Climate Impacts of Transport after the Economic Crisis*. Springer, 2010. (In press).

Raux C. The Potential for CO_2 emissions trading in transport: the case of personal vehicles and freight. *Energy Efficiency* 2010; 3: 133-48.

Raux C, Marlot G. Transport et effet de serre: un système de permis négociables appliqué aux automobilistes. *Transports* 2001; 407: 157-64.

Raux C, Marlot G. A System of Tradable CO_2 Permits Applied to Fuel Consumption by Motorists. *Transport Policy* 2005; 12: 255-65.

Salon D, Sperling D. *City Carbon Budgets: A Policy Mechanism to Reduce Vehicle Travel and Greenhouse Gas Emission*. OECD/ITF, 2008, 17 p.

SARECO. *Les droits négociables de stationnement pendulaire*. Rapport pour la DRAST. PREDIT, 2002, 60 p. + annexes.

Shoup D. *The High Cost of Free Parking*. Chicago: Planners Press, 2005.

Starkey R, Anderson K. *Domestic Tradable Quotas: a policy instrument for reducing greenhouse gas emissions from energy use*. Technical Report 39, 2005, Tyndal Center for Climate Change Research. <www.tyndall.ac.uk>

Stavins R. Transaction costs and tradable permits. *Journal of Environmental Economics and Management* 1995; 29: 133-48.

URF. *Faits et Chiffres. Statistiques du transport en France*. Paris:Union Routière de France, Septembre 2003.

Verhoef E, Nijkamp P, Rietveld P. *Tradable permits: their potential in the regulation of road transport externalities*. Amsterdam: Tinbergen Institute, 1996.

Walton W. The potential scope for the application of pollution permits to reducing car ownership in the UK. *Transport Policy* 1997; 4(2): 115-22.

Wang Q. *The use of a marketable permit system for light duty vehicle emission control*. PhD dissertation. Institution of Transportation Studies: University of California, Davis, 1992, 244 p.

Wang Q. Cost savings of using a marketable permit system for regulating light duty vehicle emissions. *Transport Policy* 1994; 1: 221-32.

Wit R, Boon B, Van Velzen A, Cames M, Deuber O, Lee D. *Giving wings to emission trading. Inclusion of aviation under the European Emission Trading System (ETS): design and impacts*. Report for the European Commission, DG Environment, 2005, 245 p.

Achevé d'imprimer par Corlet, Imprimeur, S.A.
14110 Condé-sur-Noireau
N° d'Imprimeur : 133543 - Dépôt légal : janvier 2011

Imprimé en France